TVEI at the Chan

Multilingual Matters

TVEI at the Change of Life

Edited by

David Hopkins

MULTILINGUAL MATTERS LTD
Clevedon · Philadelphia

Library of Congress Cataloging in Publication Data

TVEI at the Change of Life/edited by David Hopkins.
p. cm.
Includes bibliographic references
1. Career education — Congresses. 2. Technical education — Congresses.
3. Vocational education — Congresses. 4. Curriculum planning — Congresses.
I. Hopkins, David, 1949–.
LC1037.T87 1990
370.11'3 — dc20.

British Library Cataloguing in Publication Data

TVEI at the Change of Life.
1. Great Britain. Technical education. Technical & vocational education.
Programmes. Technical and Vocational Initiative.
I. Hopkins, David, 1949–.
373'01'13.

ISBN 1-85359-075-4
ISBN 1-85359-074-6 (pbk)

Multilingual Matters Ltd

Bank House, 8a Hill Road, Clevedon, Avon BS21 7HH, England. & 1900 Frost, Suite 101, Bristol, PA 19007, USA.

Typeset by Editorial Enterprises, Torquay, Devon.
Printed and bound in Great Britain by WBC Print Ltd, Bristol.

Contents

Acknowledgements

The original idea for the Conference emerged out of a discussion with Carol Fitz-Gibbon: my thanks to her and also to Terry McIntyre of the Training Agency, Mike Grover of Multilingual Matters and Gill Morley of the Cambridge Institute of Education for helping to translate that idea into the conference and this book. It is a pleasure to acknowledge the assistance of other Cambridge Institute of Education colleagues — Gill Abbott, Anita Chapman, Marilyn Leask and Barbara Shannon; and the chairs of the discussion groups — Lesley Holly, Peter Holly and Tony James. I am also grateful to Janet Harland, Terry McIntyre, Roy Pickup, Ray Robotham, Murray Saunders and Ruth Tenne who allowed me to persuade them to participate in the panel discussion. Finally, I am indebted to Colin McCabe who cheerfully and competently took on the daunting task of making the Keynote presentation, to the University of Twente who gave me the space to prepare the manuscript and, of course, to the contributors and participants at the Conference.

I should make it clear that although the contributions to this book were given at a conference funded by the Training Agency, the views expressed are those of the authors and do not necessarily reflect those of the Training Agency or any other Government Department.

David Hopkins

Acronyms

CDT — Craft, Design & Technology
CDT/HE — Craft, Design & Technology/Higher Education
CGLI — City & Guilds of London Institute
CPVE — Certificate of Pre-Vocational Education
DES — Department of Education & Science
ESG — Educational Support Grant
FE — Further Education
FEU — Further Education Unit
GCSE — General Certificate of Secondary Education
GRIST — Grant Related In-Service Training
INSET — In-Service Training
LAFIS — Local Authority Financial Institution System
LEA — Local Education Authority
LSE — Likelihood of Staying in Education
LEATGS — Local Education Authority Training Grant Scheme
LMS — Local Management of Schools
MSC — Manpower Services Commission
NCVQ — National Council for Vocational Qualifications
NFER — National Foundation for Educational Research
NVQ — National Vocational Qualifications
PI — Performance Indicator
PSE — Personal and Social Education
SEAC — Southern Examining Accreditation Council
TA — Training Agency
TRIST — TVEI-Related In-Service Training
TVEI — Technical and Vocational Educational Initiative
TVEI(E) — TVEI Extension
TVEI(P) — TVEI Pilot
UCCA — Universities Central Council for Administration
WRNAFE — Work Related Non-Advanced Further Education
YOP — Youth Opportunities Programme
YTS — Youth Training Scheme

1 TVEI at the Change of Life

DAVID HOPKINS
Cambridge Institute of Education

An original feature of the TVEI pilot has been the prominence given to the role of the local evaluator. In an attempt to overcome some of the decentralised and inevitably idiosyncratic tendencies inherent in the role, a series of meetings and conferences for local evaluators have been arranged irregularly by either the MSC or groups of local evaluators during the life of the pilot. Some of these meetings have had published outcomes (e.g. Hopkins, 1986; McCabe, 1986), and to these should be added the *TVEI Working Papers* (Fiddy & Stronach, 1986a, b) and books on TVEI edited by local evaluators (e.g. Gleeson, 1987). The world view of the TVEI local evaluator exemplified in these conferences and publications has tended to be characterised by methodological, ethical and small 'p' political issues. This stands in contrast to other accounts of TVEI. These include the more measured outcomes from the national evaluations of the TVEI pilot by the NFER and Leeds University (e.g. Bridgwood *et al.*, 1988, Barnes *et al.*, 1988), the series of booklets published by the Training Agency (*passim*) entitled *TVEI Developments* which contain collections of practitioner case studies, and the endless series of more popular articles and 'think-pieces' contained in the national press and educational journals (e.g. *The Independent* 23.3.89, *TVEI Insight*, Spring 1989). One of the strengths of such a diverse range of publications is that they present a view of TVEI from a variety of perspectives, demonstrating once again that no one group has a monopoly of the truth.

Most TVEI local evaluators believe, however, that they do have *a* version of the truth. As a group they have, over the past five years or so, been in a unique position to observe TVEI, reflect on its progress and to monitor the reality of curriculum change at the LEA, school/college and classroom levels. This places the local evaluator in a privileged and fortunate epistemological position. It is one that, in theory at least, gives him or her more intimate knowledge of the workings of local pilots than any national evaluation can hope to achieve, more objectivity than practitioners reporting on their own developments, and more depth than the journalist writing for a popular audience. If that is the positive side of the local evaluator's contribution, then the downside I am informed, is that local evaluators squander this unique and privileged position by esoteric and élitist arguments over ethics and method and by interfering politically and vicariously in areas they either do not understand or that are none of their business, or both. Whatever one's view of the role and utility of local evaluations and evaluators there is no doubt that they should have something to say about the substance of TVEI, about what it is, its strengths and weaknesses and the most profitable areas for development.

As TVEI approaches its change of life, with the pilot merging into extension, which in turn is being assimilated into (submerged by?) the National Curriculum, we thought it useful to hold a National Conference on the outcomes of the TVEI pilot as seen by local evaluators. As befits a mid-life crisis, the perspective was to be Janus-like, looking back over the pilot with a view to extension. The conference was held in Cambridge in November 1988, was attended by some 120 TVEI pilot and extension co-ordinators, local evaluators and others, and this book is one of the outcomes. The conference design included a keynote presentation by Colin McCabe that reviewed developments within the pilot; a series of 15 paper presentations, which focused on the themes of curriculum change, teaching and learning style, student profiling, learning from evaluation, and resource and economic implications; the papers were followed by group discussions; and the conference concluded with a panel discussion of issues raised in the previous sessions. The chapters that follow represent most of the papers presented at the conference. Before allowing the contributors to speak for themselves I should however touch on some of the themes and issues raised at the conference.

There is a rhetoric and reality problem involved in most discussions of TVEI. The two articles referred to earlier provide an excellent illustration of the point. In *The Independent* (23.3.89) Michael Durham, in an article entitled 'TVEI Reaches the Seven Year Itch', asks 'Is the Tory approach to vocational training a great white hope or a great white elephant?' He continues to argue for the latter option and concludes that:

> The sorcerer's apprentices will continue to chant their magic words, but their effect may prove to be quite different from what was expected — if, indeed, it works at all.

Even these brief quotes give an indication of the tone and intent of the article.

Contrast this with Jack Cross' account of his interview with Anne Jones, Director of Education Programmes for the Training Agency's Employment Department, the senior government official responsible for TVEI. In *TVEI Insight* 15.3.89 Jack Cross recounts Anne Jones' views on TVEI's compatability with the National Curriculum 'I welcomed the National Curriculum because it turned some of TVEI aims and principles into Law', on Teachers, 'Teachers must learn not to under-estimate themselves' and on the business community, 'But they're getting their act together'. The article concludes with another quote from Anne Jones:

> After all, we have had more effect than we could reasonably have expected but (and she insists this isn't a cop-out) please can we be judged in 1997?

I do not believe that either of these articles are much help in understanding or evaluating TVEI. But I take two lessons from these and similar contributions. The first is that TVEI has not been an 'unqualified success'. I say that because the literature on TVEI is sufficiently contradictory to suggest that, whatever the criteria employed, the initiative as a whole has not met its own admittedly very high expectations. This conclusion is inevitable, to be expected and is common to many other major curriculum changes. The second lesson is that the debate in general does not allow us sufficient critical purchase on what occurred during TVEI to take remedial action; because the debate is conducted mainly at the level of rhetoric. It was in an attempt to get below the level of rhetoric that we held the conference.

When I opened the conference by saying that the purpose of our meeting was to celebrate TVEI at its 'Change of Life', I was not implying self congratulation but celebration in the sense of performing publicly a critical open discussion on issues of importance. As I have implied above, too often discussions on TVEI are limited and insular and there is a need for a public debate. What are or should be the main features of this debate? It may be helpful to link my brief response to this question to the main sections of the book.

In the following chapter Colin McCabe elaborates on some of the main achievements of the pilot and I do not want to rehearse his comments here. Suffice it to say that I see two major outcomes. The first is that TVEI in the mid-1980s began to fundamentally change the educational agenda. In hindsight this has not been the exclusive preserve of TVEI but it did begin the trend: neither has it been entirely successful, but some of the critiques are touched on later. What it has done and continues to do, is to legitimise the idea of curriculum change, focus attention on teaching and learning style, give more status to technological subjects and to encourage developments in student assessment and curriculum evaluation. These are mainly structural changes related to organisation and curriculum of the school. The second area of achievement is in terms of student outcomes. Student outcomes are not necessarily restricted to examination results, as Carol Fitz-Gibbon points out in Chapter 10. They are, however, the most commonly measured and, because they are so tangible, they command enormous interest. It appears that TVEI has not had much impact on academic examination attainment (which it never claimed to have), but there is a striking amount of evidence from pilot evaluations of the impact of TVEI on students in the socio-emotional or affective domains. Great increases in TVEI students' ability to handle the new technology, increased confidence in social and work situations, and more ability to cope with career interviews have all been reported. Admittedly this is 'soft' data, yet its consistency across local evaluations suggests some reliability to this finding. It is also more in keeping with TVEI's stated objectives. TVEI does seem to have gone some way towards reducing the negative effects of the 'hidden curriculum'.These points are dealt with in more detail in subsequent chapters.

The contributions by Peter Smith and Elizabeth Defries and her colleagues in Section Two focus on 'Managing the Curriculum'. Peter Smith takes a resource management perspective on the ways in which the TVEI curriculum can be implemented within the context of the new Education Act and the implications of moving from Pilot to Extension. Elizabeth Defies and colleagues describe an approach to 'curriculum working groups' developed in an outer London Borough which supports curriculum and staff development and assists with curriculum implementation. Both these contributions are positive in tone and aspiration, but they should not disguise the fact that just because TVEI put the management of curriculum change on the agenda does not mean that it has solved all the problems. Ian Jamieson's critique in Chapter 13, in general, and the recent paper by Rob Fiddy & Ian Stronach (1987), in particular, point to delinquencies and aberrations in the TVEI change process. My own view is that insufficient attention has been paid to the problematic nature of implementation or the necessity for strategic dissemination, and little effort has been given to developing more sophisticated strategies for change. Change practitioners in North America have reflected on their experience of innovation in a productive way and their conclusions may be of some help to us as we continue to work in this important area (e.g. Crandall *et al.*, 1986; Fullan, 1985).

Although TVEI has given a major impetus to a re-consideration of teaching–learning style, problems of implementation and dissemination have meant that its impact on student achievement has, to date, been limited. The major problem, as the contributors to Section Three — 'Teaching and Learning Styles' attest, is that there is insufficient clarity as to the nature of what a teaching style really is. If such a specification is missing, then there is little to implement or disseminate and INSET sessions consequently become counterproductive. The recent analysis by Bruce Joyce and his colleagues (1987) demonstrates clearly that the use of well defined and specific teaching models can increase student learning, in some cases, dramatically. We also have increasingly sophisticated knowledge on how to design staff development programmes to support teaching skill acquisition by teachers (Joyce & Showers, 1988). Unfortunately, little of this knowledge or experience appears to have been applied within TVEI and, consequently, a number of promising initiatives have not fulfilled their potential. This is broadly the view taken by Martin Merson in his chapter on the 'Problem of Teaching Style in TVEI'. In it he analyses various DES and MSC documents on teaching style and finds them, at times, ambiguous and lacking in direction. He also reports some empirical findings from his evaluation of the TVEI pilot, which suggests that teachers need considerable support when adopting a new teaching strategy. This issue also contributes to the implementation problem and is in sympathy with much other research. The other two papers by Gill Davidson and Carl Parsons, and Richard Hazelwood also report on data collected during their local evaluations of TVEI. They too experienced difficulties in locating adequate operational definitions of teaching style, but despite this, did find evidence of a change in style with TVEI. They also raise some important questions about the discreteness of a TVEI approach to teaching, and the importance of teachers adopting a more flexible and experimental approach to their teaching.

Student Profiling, the focus of Section Four, is another area where TVEI has made significant progress. Although profiling is generally regarded as a 'good thing', both papers raise serious questions about the implementation and cost-benefits of profiling. John Beattie (Chapter 9) quotes the Headteacher who commented that 'God created the world in seven days but even he did not leave enough time for profiling'. Profiling, as both he and Gill Helsby (Chapter 8) point out, is extremely time-consuming to do properly and it also has repercussions on the way the curriculum is developed and taught. This raises the wider implementation issue of adopting a very complex and potentially far-reaching innovation without considering its impact on other areas of the schools curriculum and organisation. There is no doubt that TVEI has contributed substantially to the development of profiling; in extension it would do well to look more closely at some of the implementation issues.

Inevitably, and despite my earlier disclaimers, evaluators will talk about evaluation. The two papers in Section Five take different themes. In Chapter 10 Carol Fitz-Gibbon reflects on the impact that her and colleagues' paper on examination results of TVEI and non-TVEI pupils has had (Fitz-Gibbon *et al.*, 1988). She is justifiably concerned about the misinterpretation of their results and the way it was (mis)reported in the national press: again more rhetoric than reality. She then argues that any data, however unwelcome, should be regarded as formative and informative and used for developmental purposes. In Chapter 11 Denis Gleeson and his colleagues examine the main differences between evaluating TVEI as a pilot and TVEI as an extension. Their principal argument is that:

> evaluators need to position themselves to see how local management strategies and institutional practice realise and match the rhetoric of central policies and the anticipated outcomes envisaged by local education authorities.

They are ambivalent about how far the qualitative, formative and action oriented evaluation characteristic of TVEI local evaluations can survive in a context where LEAs are 'contracted to deliver specific curriculum change via the imposition of national criteria'. The experience of the local evaluation of the TVEI pilot, however, has helped evaluators and co-ordinators develop evaluation strategies to fit changing situations. My own experience in a number of LEAs entering extension suggests that such developmental work is occurring and that it can meet the demands of central and local government and the schools (Hopkins, 1989). The wealth of evaluation experience produced by the pilot represented, for example, in the 'Advisory Notes on Planning Local Evaluation under TVEI Extension' (TVEI, 1988a) and the *Local Evaluation Pack* (TVEI, 1988b) as well as the sources mentioned earlier, provide a sound basis for further development. Despite this, it is only a basis and much work remains to be done on the part of evaluators and co-ordinators if the fears of Denis Gleeson and his colleagues are not to be realised. The section concludes with a short article by Pamela Young on the importance of evaluating the financial implications of TVEI.

The final section of the book is devoted to critique. It would be foolish and misleading, as I have already pointed out, to regard the TVEI pilot as an overwhelming success. The nature of formative evaluation is that we learn through experience and the contributions by Peter Senker and Ian Jamieson are to be viewed in that light. Having said that, the perspectives of these two contributions contrast considerably. Peter Senker, in Chapter 13, takes a macro-level view of TVEI as a strand of the present government's economic policy. He argues that if:

> a diagnosis of Britain's economic problems underpinned the original conception of TVEI, then that diagnosis was seriously flawed.

This is an interesting point that Stronach (1987), among others, has made but it needs to be argued out on its own terms. The formative utility of such an argument is obviously limited, particularly as TVEI has increasingly become, even in the eyes of its originators, an educational initiative rather than a tool (if it ever really was regarded as such) of economic policy. Whatever the reasons for its inception TVEI for good or ill is with us and, as Peter Senker points out, 'TVEI resources have often been put to good purpose'. Although Senker's view of TVEI is somewhat tangential to the main theme of the book, which is devoted to gleaning educational lessons from the local evaluations of the TVEI pilot, it does point up the need for those responsible for initiating and managing TVEI policy to clarify its educational purposes and to design structures for effective implementation and evaluation. Ian Jamieson's critique reflects a more intimate knowledge of the scheme in practice. In Chapter 14 he draws together many of the issues surrounding the management of change in TVEI and outlines some serious shortcomings. A number of the points I have made in this chapter concerning implementation are developed in his analysis. In much the same way as other contributors have done in reference to more specific innovations, he argues that management structures need to be redesigned to accommodate and be receptive to curriculum change, rather than forcing new curriculum developments into existing structures. He concludes, for example that:

> the national curriculum must mean that much of TVEI must be delivered horizontally across the curriculum . . . . This will be difficult where the major organisational structures, the departments, are vertically organised.

These then are some of the main issues around which the public debate on TVEI needs to be conducted. It is a sign of maturity that the issues now at stake are to do with management and implementation rather than on the substance of the programmes themselves. As TVEI moves through its change of life, it is instructive to realise that there is no longer a debate on its principles and aims, which appeared so contentious to so many only five or six years ago.

References

BARNES, D. *et al.* 1988, *A Second Report on the TVEI Curriculum*. London: TVEI, Training Commission.

BRIDGWOOD, A. *et al.* 1988, *Perspectives on TVEI: Management Themes*. London: TVEI, Training Commission.

CRANDALL, D. *et al.* 1986, Strategic planning issues that bear on the success of school improvement efforts. *Educational Administration Quarterly* 22 (3), 21–53.

FIDDY, R. & STRONACH, I. (eds) 1986 a & b, *TVEI Working Papers 1 & 2*. Norwich: CARE, UEA (for the MSC).

— 1987, Fables and futures: Cases in the management of innovation. In D. GLEESON (ed.), *TVEI and Secondary Education*. Milton Keynes: Open University Press.

FITZ-GIBBON, C. *et al.* 1988, Performance indicators and the TVEI pilot. *Evaluation and Research in Education* 2 (2), 49–60.

FULLAN, M. 1985, Change processes and strategies at the local level. *The Elementary School Journal* 85 (3), 391–421.

GLEESON, D. 1987, *TVEI and Secondary Education*. Milton Keynes: Open University Press.

HOPKINS, D. 1986, *TVEI: Some Methodological Issues*. Cambridge: Cambridge Institute of Education (for the MSC).

— 1989, *Evaluation for School Development*. Milton Keynes: Open University Press.

Independent, The 1989, TVEI reaches the seven year itch (article by M. Durham). Tuesday, 23 March.

JOYCE B. *et al.* 1987, Staff development and student learning: a synthesis of research on models of teaching. *Educational Leadership* 5 (2), 11–23.

JOYCE B. and SHOWERS, B. 1988, *Student Achievement Through Staff Development*. New York: Longman Inc.

MCCABE, C. (ed.) 1986, *TVEI: The Organisation of the Early Years*. Clevedon, Avon: Multilingual Matters.

STRONACH, I. 1987, Ten years on. *Forum* 29 (3), 64–66.

TRAINING AGENCY (passim) *TVEI Developments* (a series of booklets Nos 1–8). London: Training Agency.

TVEI EVALUATION UNIT 1988a, Advisory Notes on Planning Local Evaluation under the TVEI Extension. London: MSC (mimeo).

— 1988b, Local evaluation: Some lessons from the Pilot. London: MSC (mimeo).

TVEI Insight 1989, Talking to the Director (account of an interview by J. Cross). No. 15, Spring.

2 Evaluating TVEI: What we have learned

COLIN McCABE
School of Education, University of Newcastle

It is five years since the first projects of the initiative were introduced into schools and four years since the main bulk were started — the school life of one pupil from fourteen to eighteen. The aims were 'to explore and test ways of organising and managing the education of 14–18 year old young people across the ability range' so as to bring about certain stated outcomes. These testings and explorations were to be undertaken 'in such a way that . . . emphasis was placed on careful monitoring and evaluation (and) individual projects were managed at local level'. This quite bold, highly significant combination of national initiative with local responsibility is what we are here to review from the point of view of the local evaluations which were so forward-looking a part of this innovation.

Since I have had both the opportunity and facilities to look generally at what has come out of all this work I now believe that such a review is both necessary and timely in these closing stages of the pilot projects. I think that the messages which are identifiable from this overview give us a direction for future development and remind us that this is indeed merely 'the end of the beginning' — the real work still lies ahead.

The British secondary and further education systems are big, longstanding and complex. Even the relatively impressive resources and the most enthusiastic efforts of TVEI can change relatively little in five years. In the early years perhaps some of us were a little blinded by our enthusiasm and even over-stimulated by rhetoric so that we thought that we were already changing the world. Now that we can look realistically at what has resulted we must not feel let down or disappointed. A very good start has been made. The enthusiasm and the rhetoric were essential to that start as they are to the efforts of all reformers but now we look at the lessons provided by the monitoring of the pilot schemes and see what we need to do now that they cease to be pilots — the pilots are dropped and the main voyages begin.

As a keynote I go back to something which was published 66 years ago for there is little really new in the recurring themes of education, as Mathieson & Bernbaum's recent paper (1988) may remind us — too pessimistically in this context. A range of discussions with individuals currently involved with TVEI evaluation reminded me of a theme which I could neither quite remember nor recall. It seemed to run through so many of the messages coming out of evaluations currently and eventually took me back to the old lessons in A. N. Whitehead's '*Aims of Education*' (1929). He took Hegel's analysis of progress into three stages — Thesis, Antithesis and Synthesis and applied his ideas to educational theory. The terms which Whitehead used for the stages he identified in intellectual progress were the stage of romance, the stage of precision and the stage of generalisation. I hope that I am not unduly bending the evidence we now have before us when I suggest that much of it indicates that we are now leaving or have recently left the stage of romance in TVEI — the heady enthusiastic, trying-things-out years of the initiative and its corresponding monitoring. We are entering or have entered the state of precision — a stage for more tactical targeting than creative innovation.

It might have been hoped that by now we should have been at the stage of generalisation but I do not think that the evidence points that way. We are in the position of someone who has just learned to handle some complex piece of high technology equipment — say a new flying machine. We have been enthusiastic about it, we have tried it in many situations and we know that it works — we must not underestimate how new it is and how much it can do. Now we have got to learn to use it seriously, and tactically to reach accepted and agreed targets in education. This applies to evaluation and to projects themselves.

I state an extreme case here. An enthusiastic, possibly although not necessarily young teacher, has introduced a new, originally cross-curricular subject using innovative approaches. Four years of effort and development produce something promising and reasonably established. He or she still has to compete with or be compared with their classics colleagues with centuries of back-up and half a century of developed, targeted, successful teaching and learning approaches and skills. It is now that the support structures, the networks to under-pin good practice, the aids to targeting are going to have to be identified and provided for the innovative teacher. To overstate the case still further, generalised heroism and enthusiasm are not enough (Britons were supposed to have learned that at the Battle of the Somme), selection, precise identification and application of what has been achieved, tactically applied, could be the way forward at this stage.

This, then, I suggest to you as a theme for what follows as I try to give a broad picture from the monitoring so far undertaken. If anyone is inclined to ask whether the stage of romance could in this case have been shortened I am inclined to think not. It is always an essential stage to be worked through in any cycle. Perhaps the messages were there a year or so ago but individuals have indeed been moving towards greater precision and effectiveness in that time. The important thing seems to be that, as always, we move forward from where we are, both in the pilot schools and in the colleges and schools undertaking the extension.

The headings for the broad picture are:

a) Overview of the pilot evaluation.
b) Some problems of the local evaluation.
c) What has been learned.
d) How can this help with future development?

Overview of the Pilot Evaluation

The monitoring and evaluation processes established by the then Manpower Services Commission at the start of the projects were more comprehensive than for any previous national trial of an educational innovation. The two national commissioned evaluations in the areas of changes in organisation and teaching (NFER and Leeds University) were complemented by a comprehensive monitoring of statistics carried out by the central unit in collaboration with Trent Polytechnic for Curriculum and the NFER for Student Databases. These activities made schools and authorities aware of the national interest in and significance of their work and served as a reminder to them of their contractual status. Their outcomes are nationally valuable and will be of great use in future planning or debate but have not, in general, been able to provide or feedback information or conclusions quickly enough to meet the more pressing needs and discussions of individual schools and local authorities. It has been found, too, in other contexts, that the evaluation of programmes as opposed to individual projects can easily lead to their having different (and certainly less flexible) objectives.

Naturally I am biased but the establishing of local evaluations of individual projects seems to have been one of the MSC's best moves. The method of its funding (it had to be arranged and commissioned by each individual LEA) was well thought out, promoting as it did an on-going relationship between LEAs, schools and evaluators which could respond rapidly to the development of the projects. Ownership lay with the authorities and the teachers. This established, in the best cases, ideas and principles of co-operative evaluation within and across schools and colleges. Some of these partners proved to be incompatible but most found that there could be a developing interaction between evaluators and schools, often following a pattern from the general to the particular, from early description to later analysis, from the evaluator having little in the way of a brief to their latterly being asked to undertake precise tasks. When used in this way the local evaluation could properly be seen as an embryonic structure supporting and guiding change and perhaps this is how it should be seen in the future.

Different patterns of relationships have been tried — individuals being directly commissioned by one or more authorities, teams usually based on higher education institutions working across a group of authorities or teams similarly based working individually with authorities. Each arrangement can work well but in most cases an authority, it seems, wants to recognise an individual as responsible and responsive to them while the level of funding available is enough to pay only about 20% of a salary — but this is one of the recurring problems of evaluation and costing in education generally.

I have written elsewhere of the more precise definition of evaluation which authorities are moving towards through these experiences (McCabe, 1987). Do you, in future, want your evaluator to monitor your performance indicators or to act as a consultant? And if the latter, is he or she to act as a general guide or to be retained only for specific items?

Some Problems of the Local Evaluation

Fiddy & Stronach (1987) wrote with feeling and at some length last year of the problems of making formative evaluation effective. We all remember the painstaking report which an authority did not even acknowledge.

I was wrong a few years ago when I wrote that local authorities were then experienced in evaluation and ready for more (McCabe, 1986). It proved that this was probably only true in INSET terms. Neither LEAs nor their evaluators knew what evaluation could do in the new context so that working out the appropriate relationship with each LEA has not always been easy on either side. Only now perhaps do you as LEAs know what you want us for — and you do not always like the outcomes. Allowing a semi-independent stranger to range at large in your schools can disturb your system.

It is rather important for the evaluator to know:

— Who is to decide what should be evaluated?
— Who is it for? (Is the evaluator to be the co-ordinator's assistant? — or the deputy director's?)
— How independent is the evaluation to be?
— What does independence mean in this context?
— Who approves the reports?
— Who sees the reports? (Who are the audience?)
— Who owns the reports?
— Who decides what schools, what teachers, what pupils the evaluator sees?
— In future, should we be dealing with individual schools rather than authorities?

Finally in this section I return to the question of why you bring in someone from outside at all. In the past five years internal evaluation has grown apace. The conversation of advisers and deputy heads is full of activities which they have evaluated or audited. This is excellent for it is professional activity at its fullest and a benefit largely of TVEI. Why then do you decide to bring in (and pay at realistic rates) someone from outside? As a hallmark, possibly, 'We have so and so who evaluates our project for us . . .', but more practically either because the matter is better dealt with by someone disinterested or it needs expertise which is not internally available or it calls for a service more efficiently and economically provided across authorities. In any case it means that evaluation should be more targeted and defined. What should the evaluator — from outside — now be called? A consultant? An overviewer? How far can his or her role be validly taken on by someone whose employment and career depend upon the authority or the project itself?

What has been Learned?

The answer first of all must be that most of the local evaluator's activity, like that of the teacher or the co-ordinator, never appears in the literature or any report. When you ask your evaluator to go round the schools and report on progress towards some favoured objective we all realise that he or she is largely promoting that aspect of the project for you and at the same time giving your colleagues in schools opportunities to sort out their ideas and express their interest. The value of having an evaluator has indeed been learned by many co-ordinators, even when the comments fed back home often had to be less optimistic than an enthusiastic leader had expected.

The collected reports of local evaluation record the general trials and efforts of all the projects towards achieving the aims of the initiative — the inevitably patchy but conscientious moves towards equal opportunities, the active, rapidly changing, scene of information technology and its growing influence across the curriculum, the mixed success of movements made in profiling, the progress towards integrating the new complementary or supplementary elements of the 16 to 18 curriculum and the changes which teachers (and their pupils) report in teaching styles. Teachers feel that they have been given considerable freedom to change and experiment but it is sometimes questioned whether the support structures give sufficient direction and opportunity for more than a process of diffusion to occur. Some identify the sort of centralised structures which most effectively support change. Much of this is represented in subsequent papers for this conference. In some cases — I think here of students with special needs — TVEI has filled gaps and provided much wanted opportunity, in others it has given helpful chances to try new administrative approaches — these, perhaps being less documented than they should be because of the level at which evaluation generally occurred.

An interesting further illustration of the power of local evaluation organisation is given by the rapidity with which they can collect and process good quality performance indicators for authorities. This quantitative aspect of local evaluation has been a minor part of pilot activities but is of growing importance.

Three papers which have become available recently are particularly helpful in considering outcomes. They are:

(i) Gill Helsby & Murray Saunders report on 'School to Work' from Lancaster — quoted in the '*Insight*' journal (1988). This report, based on 3,000 16–17-year-olds across 14 LEAs, reports how positively they reflect upon their pilot TVEI experiences. So many young people too have welcomed the extra work experience provided by TVEI it is good that it has been so well described. (See Table 2.1.)

TABLE 2.1 *Proportions of TVEI and non-TVEI students agreeing to statements about their fifth form studies*

	ex-TVEI students %	*non-TVEI students* %
The work I did in the fifth form helped to teach me the skills I need to find a job.	41.8	31.7
The work I did in the fifth form helped to teach me the skills I need in a job.	40.1	26.9
The work I did in the fifth form helped me to understand what it would be like when I go to work.	33.7	17.3
The work I did in the fifth form helped me to find out which job I would be best at.	33.3	29.3
Most of what I did in the fifth form was a waste of time.	17.5	18.7
The work I did in the fifth form helped me to learn to get on with other people.	65.2	56.0
The work I did in the fifth form helped me to understand things like taxes, bank accounts, how to fill in forms and that kind of thing.	59.4	39.6
The work I did in the fifth form helped me to use things like computers.	74.0	43.6

(*Source*: Helsby & Saunders, 1988)

(ii) Rob Fiddy's final report on TVEI in Essex and Suffolk (August 1988) is a useful source of discussion and ideas on planning. For me the two emphases which are most significant are that on the need to encourage and recognise the individuality of institutions within a project — 'A school within a project situation is recommended rather than attempting to establish a project within schools' — and the identification of student centred learning as 'that mode of teaching which is the most effective form within the situation.' The need for more detailed action research is stressed while some failed experiments are acknowledged, hopefully for further progress.

(iii) The third paper in its conclusions starts from a similar 'much more concentrated effort on developing strategies for pupil-centred learning' for its own purposes. Julie Howard & David Hopkins' study of 'Information Skills in TVEI and the role of the librarian' (1988) might not be the first title one would turn to for general guidance on TVEI but its conclusions, issues and guidelines are highly pertinent. They cover the whole field of how to move from a situation of isolated, un-coordinated examples of excellent work — the consequence of wider initiatives — towards providing an infrastructure for teaching skills and strategies.

How far all the original objectives of the Initiative have been achieved nation-wide it is hard — and perhaps too early — to see, the best should be still to come, but a good local evaluation is well informed about and has insight into what have been the most important and significant outcomes in its own area. These turn out to be rather different from the first objectives but show how these projects have led the way and prepared the ground for so much later innovation. When we look at these effects we realise what a powerful and innovative force TVEI has been — and I suggest that only semi-independent local evaluation can recognise and describe this at the appropriate level.

How Can this Help with Future Development?

A first point to make, from what has gone before, is that in this section I am clearly not thinking of the 'extension' alone. The messages in the first place are for the pilot schools which are already so far on the way towards 'getting it right' but need the support and encouragement of an infrastructure which can enable them to identify and have faith in their individual strengths and successes — and work on them until they are reliable and replicable as well as being valid. To be told in a school that 'the 14 to 16 pilot is dead' by a frustrated teacher indicates a neglect and lack of understanding of how teaching develops on someone's part and a major sacrifice of effort.

There is a good deal of debate about the focus of the extension. Can it be authority wide. Should it be the responsibility of the schools? Do consortia work? An answer seems to be that schools with independent responsibility working together in consortia is a promising mode — schools have gained a great deal through working together and knowing what each other is doing in the pilot scheme. But the emphasis is on working together, not on having formal meetings at a surface level. The contact would be through working groups identifying and developing success in detail, making it practicable and replicable. A central support team, probably home grown in response to growing need seems necessary. You may interpret the messages differently.

The key message that the — no longer new — curriculum areas now need targeting, sharpening and applying throughout the system seems to be clearer. Is a further message that small is beautiful?

The parallel message for evaluation is also one which aims at precision. An analysis is needed in each authority of what can validly be done by those running a project — the co-ordinator's own evaluation must be highly professionally valuable and necessary even if methodologically suspect. Where an individual or organisation outside the authority is called in, the scope of the contract should be agreed in some detail, as any firm would expect from a consultant making a proposal. And the individual or organisation is professionally responsible for the outcome. An individual must be responsible for the quality and consequences. This service or expertise is what you are paying for so the analysis and negotiation stages are more important now, to both parties, than they were at the start of the pilot project. If you expect the production of performance indicators, is this partly to help you develop your own system in future years— you will want to second colleagues to learn the business? If your adviser colleagues stress illuminative evaluation how closely can this be looked at?

Even though David Hopkins has organised this conference I must refer to his paper published by the Training Agency and now further available in the journal *Evaluation and Research in Education*(Hopkins, 1988). This, the outcome of a good deal of combined experience in local evaluation, was produced in the fourth year of the pilot in the hope that it could help the extension start from 'where we are'. It gives a highly adaptable plan for using evaluation as a parallel scheme to innovation. This may seem idealistic but it can, he suggests, be used at almost any level to give structure and an analytic base to any form of local evaluation. It is worth considering.

And I hope this at least prepares you for what follows.

References

FIDDY, R. 1988, TVEI in Essex and Suffolk. CARE, University of East Anglia (mimeo).

FIDDY, R. & STRONACH, I. 1987, How can evaluation become formative. CARE, University of East Anglia (mimeo).

HELSBY, G. & SAUNDERS, M. 1988, School to work: The difference that TVEI makes. IRDPCE, University of Lancaster (mimeo). (Summary in *TVEI Insight* No.14 Autumn 1988.)

HOPKINS, D. 1988, Evaluating for development. *Evaluation and Research in Education* 2 (1), 1–10.

HOWARD, J. & HOPKINS, D. 1988, Information skills in TVEI and the role of the librarian. *British Library Report* No.51.

McCABE, C. (ed.), 1986, *TVEI: The Organisation of the Early Years*. Clevedon, Avon: Multilingual Matters.

— 1987, The external evaluator — Inspector or management consultant? *Evaluation & Research in Education* 1(1), 1–8.

MATHIESON, M. & BERNBAUM, G. 1988, The British disease: A British tradition. *British Journal of Educational Studies*, 36 (2), 126–74.

WHITEHEAD, A. N. 1929, *Aims of Education*. London: Williams and Norgate.

3 Resource management and TVEI: Implications for schools and colleges

PETER SMITH
Northampton LEA TVEI Director

TVEI and a Changing Educational Culture

In the early days of TVEI one was often reminded by our advisers from MSC that we *must not forget* our contractual obligation to ensure that we *tested and explored ways of managing the curriculum* to deliver certain outcomes *as cost effectively as possible to a named cohort*. With the Extension of TVEI the same wording is present in the criteria in terms of cost effectiveness and during the life of TVEI a number of key phrases surface ever more frequently among the various educational discussions — performance indicators, efficiency and effectiveness, unit costs, budget management and so on. There is then a more distinct orientation to the notion of an input–output model of accountability, particularly from those civil servants within the Training Agency and our friends in the Audit Commission. With the introduction of the Local Management of Schools scheme with its delegated budgets, where the governing body and the headteachers will have freedom to deploy resources within the schools budget according to their own educational needs and priorities, the accent is on the *total* management process of relating resources to the curriculum. Certain items of revenue are, however, to be retained under LEA control, one of which is TVEI funding which is clarified as 'earmarked' resourcing, to ensure strategic change.

What I want to share with you are thoughts as to TVEI's position in the context of the Education Reform Act (1988), and the implications of moving from Pilot to Extension.

In so doing I present a model which illustrates the various interactions that must be managed by schools, colleges and LEAs, analyse its particular components and consider the implications for schools and colleges in terms of managing their resources, both human, physical and financial.

The Accountability Model

The model shows the interaction of four elements — resources, the curriculum, staff development and students. What the accountability argument suggests is that effective and efficient management of the range of inputs and interactions will produce improved student outcomes, which we should and can identify through a range of performance indicators. Hence in the model (see Figure 3.1) a number of sectors can be defined to provide 'windows' into the workings of the model.

Framework Model

Central to the model is the notion that our total effort is aimed at the improvement of the quality of learning for pupils and students. Hence the management of the various inputs leads to quality performance that can be recognised and articulated to a range of partners of consumers.

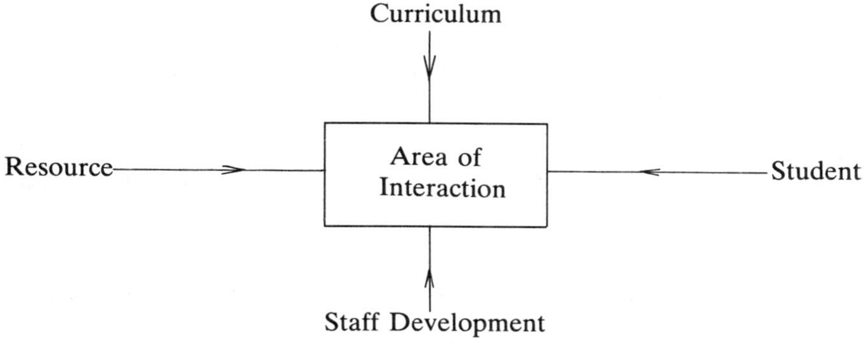

Area of Interaction houses the mix of inputs that lead to quality if properly managed. Indicators of performance arise from the interaction.

FIGURE 3.1 *The national curriculum and TVEI*

	Maths	Eng	Sci	Hist	Geog	Tech	Music	Art	P.E.	Lang			
Equal Opportunities													
Industry Links													
Information Technology													
Economic Awareness													
Enterprise													
Personal Effectiveness (PSE)													
Technology													
Experiential Learning													
Problem Solving													
Management of Own Learning													
Careers Guidance Inc. Work Exp.													
Records Of Achievement													

Application of the Model

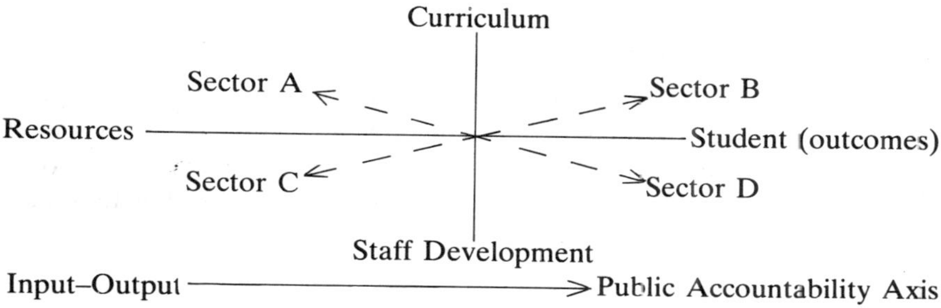

When we apply the model there is a clear relationship between sectors to indicate effectiveness and efficiency. From this there can be produced a classification of indicators that provide 'ways in' to self evaluation and provide a rationale for monitoring, inspection, and evaluation.

Sector A

Leads to the analysis of the application of Resources to the curriculum and their usage both from an efficiency and effectiveness viewpoint, for example:

- Costs of equipment; equipment/room usage; staff/student ratios; relative balance of resources between curriculum areas.
- Curriculum planning.

Sector B

Leads to an evaluation that is student/teacher centred with reference to factors such as:

- Validity of curriculum objectives.
- Profiling, Record of Achievement and curriculum review.
- Student perceptions of curriculum.
- Assessment of performance.

Sector C

Could be applied in a number of ways both quantitatively and qualitatively to show the effectiveness of the planning of staff development and the application of resources, e.g. secondments.

Sector D

Leads to an evaluation of the outcomes of the application of resources on student outcomes through:

— Evaluation of staff development programmes and impact on student learning.
— Teacher appraisal.
— Methods of staff development.

What is now taking place within LEAs, schools and colleges is a close analysis of the implications of the new Act in relation to the National Curriculum and in the context of the Local Management of Schools (LMS). What follows is analysis of the delivery of TVEI within that context, using the model (Figure 3.1) as a framework.

TVEI and the Curriculum

Firstly one must identify what is meant by TVEI in relation to the whole curriculum before one can really begin to consider the implications for the management of resources. In the early days of pilot projects teachers, advisers, officers, industrialists and parents strove to identify what TVEI was, indeed still do. There is a view that there are as many views as to what TVEI is as there are projects actively promoting it. However, evaluators have examined the plethora of versions and identified a number of common elements. It would seem that there has been a tendency to move through three phases, namely:

(i) a promotion of pre-vocational/vocational courses, arising from an option culture.
(ii) a pre-occupation with a technological element.
(iii) an identification with 'threads and processes' to provide balance and breadth in the National Curriculum.

(i) Pre-vocational courses

1983/84 was, as we can now see, the ending of the era of the option culture, but one in which TVEI was often offered as an option on the timetable for the cohort. It was 30% of the timetable for a fixed number of students, for whom additional resources were provided. Curriculum plans for this were produced on one side of A4, showing in bold type the TVEI options — electronics; control technology; business studies — and each year the curriculum data base was fed with statistics on student take-up of the various options and the resultant print-outs indicated the 'performance' of schools in promoting TVEI courses and curriculum change.

(ii) A technological element

A number of significant changes began to emerge as the focus on the Technological element increased, not only because of the increasing pre-occupation with the problem — 'What is Technology?' but also how could one achieve progression and maintain equality of opportunity in terms of gender. Increasingly issues of 'process' dominated the TVEI debate and the notion of a 30% subject enclave within the curriculum gave way to a more pervasive view of TVEI. The dedication of resources to the fulfillment of these notions, becomes more problematic as does the notion of performance indicators.

(iii) Threads and processes

With the introduction of the National Curriculum and TVEI Extension debate has intensified from two standpoints, one the time allocation per subject argument and the second the preservation of balance. What has been articulated is the notion that TVEI is concerned with the cross-curricular processes that stem from the TVEI core and the curriculum criteria, namely:

Technology and Information Technology
Careers Guidance
Experience of Work and Industry Links
Economic Awareness
Profiling and Records of Achievement
Equality of Opportunity
Progression
Personal Effectiveness

Hence the curriculum model had become one of subjects and threads (see Figure 3.2).

In terms of the management of resources three dominant issues emerge, namely:

(i) What will be the consequence of having a curriculum where certain studies — Business Studies, Computer Studies, Home Economics — do not have a place in the National Curriculum on a *subject basis*?
(ii) What should TVEI resource in terms of the development and delivery of Technology.
(iii) What are the consequences of the new curriculum model for school management, in particular the role and status of a TVEI Co-ordinator?

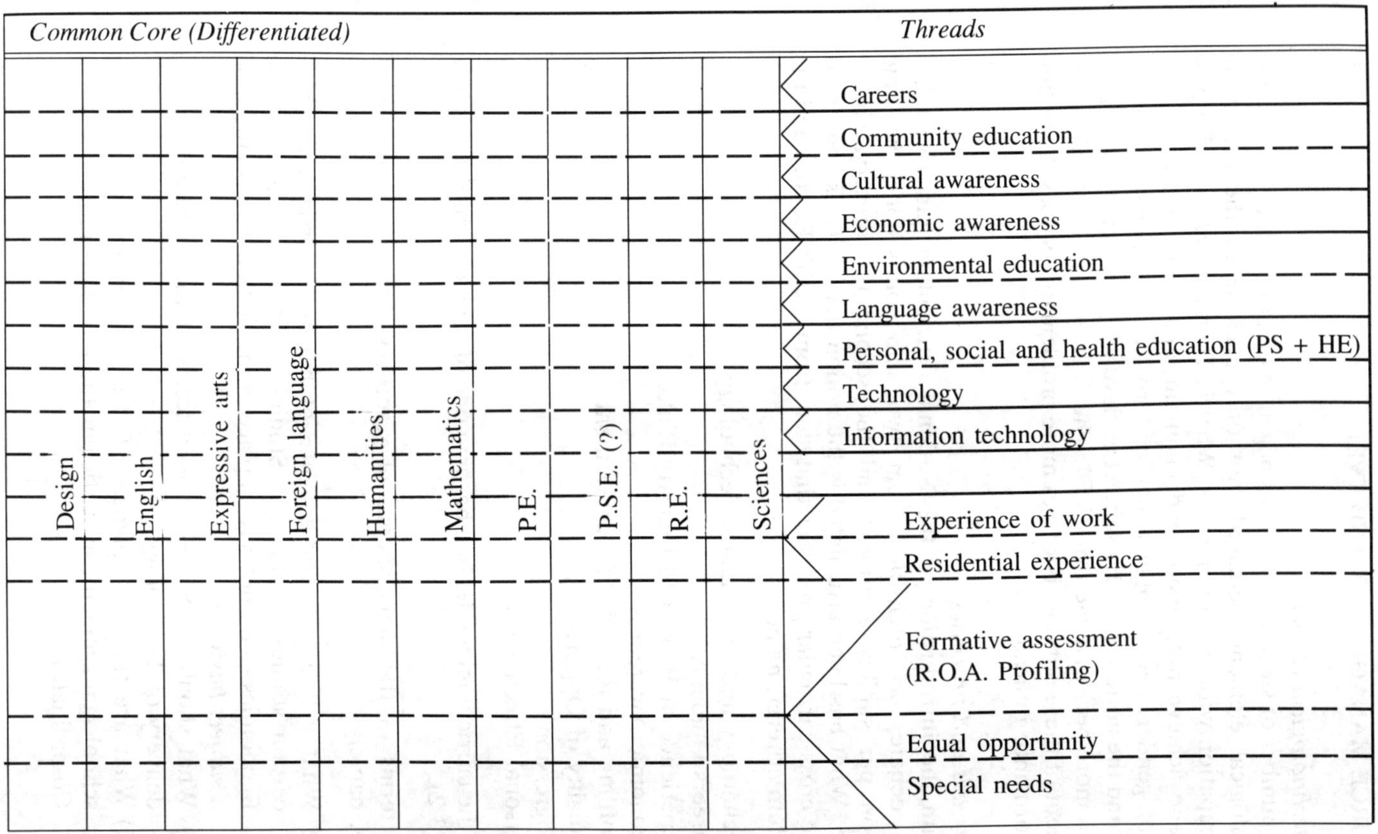

Note: Up to 20% 'free' options in addition to the above in 4th and 5th years

FIGURE 3.2 *Model for a 11–16 curriculum*

Staff Development

Under the TVEI Pilot and Extension Budgets there is a heading for 'Training' which has taken on a number of different meanings, with different emphases as we have gone through the past five years. In a sense three activities have been inter-related — curriculum development; associated staff development; and training.

However, in tracing the general developments within TVEI there has been a tendency for:

(i) Projects to be somewhat isolated from mainstream LEA development.
(ii) The focus to be on new ways of organising and delivering the curriculum — witness the number of modular schemes.
(iii) Accent on exploring effective methods of large scale staff development and avoiding disruption of student learning.

With the Extension of TVEI and its clearer focus in terms of the National Curriculum there is a need to consider the implications of managing 'staff training and development' in relation to three other 'strategic' instruments at the disposal of government and LEAs, namely:

The Local Authority Training Grant Scheme (LEATGS)
Educational Support Grants (ESGs)
Work Related Non-Advanced Further Education (WRNAFE)

These three, together with TVEI, form the strategic development mechanisms to implement national change. Clearly there are under the new act and with Local Management of Schools and Colleges critical questions to ask and answer in terms of the inter-relationships of these four instruments of change, namely:

(i) What are the distinct contributions of each of the four 'instruments', particularly where they may overlap, for example the development, delivery and training for Information Technology?
(ii) How is funding to be delegated or retained within the LEA with reference to schools, colleges, consortia and the provision of advisory support staff?
(iii) How is the use of such funding to be monitored, what performance indicators should apply and how can the relative or comparative performances of the different mechanisms be appraised?

(iv) How do we deploy staff development money to ensure collaborative development between schools and colleges at a time when the new Act *appears* to promote greater individual school/college autonomy?

In terms of the management of the LEA, consortia, schools and colleges there are profound implicatins for the need for closer integration at all levels.

At school or college level the distinctive labels applied to particular post holders — Professional Development Tutor; TVEI Co-ordinator; CPVE Co-ordinator; coupled with manner in which such posts were created tends to lead to a somewhat uncoordinated approach.

For some Pilot schools there is also the added difficulty of promoting a whole school approach where there has been a strong TVEI enclave.

TVEI's particular contribution to the National Curriculum and possibly even more significantly to the post-16 sector emphasises the balancing and pervasive processes. Hence a clear and balanced view of the total inter-relationships of the four strategic funding mechanisms is important for all teachers to understand.

Resource Management

In the preceding sections on curriculum and staff development two aspects have been examined, namely TVEI's relationship with the National Curriculum and with other instruments of national change. In this section we look at the implications for management of TVEI resourcing, again in the context of what has happened in the pilot and what issues we must address in the extension in the context of the new Act.

TVEI Pilot Projects housed within them a microcosm of the new educational culture by offering opportunities for schools and colleges to engage in innovation within prescribed criteria and in part be responsible for their resourcing in cash terms. What projects had to engage in was the formulation and trialing of curriculum ideas and their evaluation. In terms of resourcing, therefore the Pilot Project provided 'sufficient' resources to promote development, delivery of aspects of the curriculum with smaller groups of pupils, equipment, premises adaptation, staff development and the funding of school/college links.

It led to the concept of a 'fairly self-sufficient project, small control teams, school and college co-ordinators and somewhat separate developments in terms of whole LEA or whole school.'

TVEI Extension funding is far less per capita than the Pilot — in Northants £2 million over 5 years for 960 pupils — £2,000 per pupil for the Pilot whereas the Extension over 7 years is £8.5 million for 40,000 pupils or £200 per pupil. (Figures are approximate.) Consequently in terms of TVEI and the National Curriculum and for the 16–18 phase the focus for the application of the funding becomes sharper and must be considered in the light of other funding. The primary purpose is for *development* not *delivery*.

In terms of the Local Management of Schools LEAs are required to apply a formula for school budgets based on per pupil/capita cost per annum. In other words one is moving to notions of unit costing which headteachers and managers of the education service will embrace out of necessity.

In terms of strategic funding, including TVEI, we must attempt to deliver a curriculum that is 'cost effective'. An example of unit costing could be applied to Work Experience where for a three week placement the cost per pupil in terms of placement agency and teacher preparation/briefing time could be £45, excluding industry's costs. Such unit costs will inevitably be produced or attempted for those curriculum elements that TVEI is aimed at developing and delivering.

Three questions have to be asked, in the light of the curriculum model and the total 14–18 development.

(i) What is TVEI actually funding — development or delivery of the curriculum?
(ii) If TVEI is contributing to the development of an 'entitlement' curriculum how will it be maintained after funding ceases?
(iii) How is the staffing money to be deployed during the Extension Phase?

It would seem the primary function of the funding is to assist in strategic development, as translated within the school, colleges and the LEA.

In terms of school management the notion of a 'co-ordinator' as developed under the pilot would seem a redundant concept. To deliver TVEI in relation to the curriculum model requires a senior management team approach to look at the whole curriculum and delegate particular functions to a range of staff.

In terms of a five year phase of Extension Development short term development targets require identification and specific remuneration — targeted funding for specific objectives. At consortia and LEA level the deployment of advisory/central TVEI support is critical. If TVEI is assisting in the provision of the 'threads and processes' then LEAs must aggregate fractions of the resources from the various strategic monies to ensure coherent approaches, for example central groups to address Records of Achievement. Unit costs will then be reduced and duplication avoided.

The alternative is for TVEI to narrow its focus, for example, to Work Experience and Industry Links and pay for their delivery.

Student-Outcomes-Evaluation and Performance Indicators

Related to student outcomes is the process of accountability, evaluation and performance indicators. All the factors considered so far should lead to better student performance, which should be capable of some degree of quantification and evaluation. Under the TVEI pilot a number of measures have been used:

— numbers of pupils taking particular subjects
— destinations of students, post-16
— numbers of pupils on work experience
— numbers of certificates or qualifications gained.

However, under TVEI Extension and the new Act a number of factors, hitherto fairly low profile, will throw into sharp relief the efficiency and effectiveness arguments in terms of student outcomes, not least the process of national testing and attainment targets.

As the move to increased monitoring of performance gathers momentum a number of inter-related issues emerge, as highlighted from the experience of the past few years, namely:-

How will teachers react to 'efficiency style' performance indicators related to unit costs?
Can we find valid measures to indicate the impact of staff development programmes on student outcomes?
Can we appraise effectively the quality of management structures and processes in achieving improved student performance?
What impact will this approach have on the style of work carried out

by Local Inspectorate Services?
Can we determine whether TVEI has succeeded or failed in delivering its goods?

In this short chapter the main implications of TVEI in the new educational scene have been sketched and much work remains on how they will be addressed. It would seem the following questions have to be addressed effectively at all levels within the education service.

(i) Bearing in mind that TVEI covers the 14–18 sector and is concerned with whole curriculum processes, what are the implications for organisational structures and processes?
(ii) What are the implications of 'unit costing' and LMS formula for the allocation of TVEI resourcing?
(iii) How are schools and the LEA to be evaluated in terms of the delivery of TVEI, bearing in mind its increasing association and integration with other strategic instruments?

Note

1. The author recognises that the pace of recent developments has meant that Figures 3.1 and 3.2 have since been modified or superceded.

4 Curriculum development in TVEI: Curriculum working groups

ELIZABETH DEFRIES, MARILYN GOODMAN
London Borough of Harrow,
and JANET HARLAND
University of London Institute of Education

This chapter concerns an outer London borough in the third year of its TVEI pilot programme. Five schools have been involved and the first intake moved into the authority's three tertiary colleges in September 1988. The chapter itself draws upon a local evaluation report, produced by the authority's own Educational Research Unit with some support from an external consultant from the University of London Institute of Education. It is written jointly by the part-time research assistant appointed to the TVEI evaluation, the LEA's Educational Research Officer, and the external consultant. The report deals only with the schools, because it emerges from an evaluation study undertaken at the end of the second year of the scheme. Its topic is the inter-school curriculum working groups set up and running at various times since the scheme was agreed with the MSC. We would suggest that it is interesting to a wider audience because of the importance as well as the difficulty of such co-operative work between institutions and across sectors, not only for TVEI but for curriculum development in general.

To understand the particular function of these groups, it is necessary to place the authority's scheme on the continuum, widely debated by TVEI commentators, which runs all the way from the heavily centralised to the totally devolved. This scheme lies somewhere around the mid-point, with a tendency towards devolution. Thus, although it was agreed that the aims of the scheme should be centrally determined (and indeed, heavily influenced by national criteria), and although it was required that all the participating schools should offer options under the common headings of

World of Technology and World of Business, supporting them with a core course of school-developed modules, nevertheless it was seen as both the responsibility and the right of individual schools to find their own routes towards the common goals. This approach is consistent with the LEA's practice of not exerting a particularly directive influence over the curriculum, although the advent of the Education Reform Act is inevitably resulting in the development of a more explicit policy.

It is only with the accumulated experience of the first two years of TVEI, possibly focused through the process of evaluation, that those concerned have come to regard the devolution/centralisation issue as one which is inevitably posed by the scheme; and that at least for some specific elements within the scheme, it is one which needs to be resolved, though not necessarily in the same way on each occasion. Within the TVEI scheme itself, the role of the central team was deliberately conceived in terms of leadership and support; there has never been an intention to run a strongly centralised scheme. Indeed, so far this would have been very difficult: within the first two years there have been two co-ordinators, with a six-month inter-regnum between them. Added to this, the original plan for a central support team of three 'curriculum leaders' plus three support teachers plus an administrator has never been realised: for various reasons, no support teachers have been appointed and for a long period there was no administrator. The opportunity for the curriculum leaders to be directly interventionist has therefore been limited, not only by the difficulties inherent in their role (which we refer to later), but also by the fact that they were over-extended.

Thus we can discern a three-pronged strategy to meet the MSC's stated aim that TVEI should enable LEAs to explore and test new ways of organising and managing the education of 14–18-year-old people: firstly, a commitment by the schools to take on new curriculum aims, content and structures; secondly, a central team to guide, support and succour; and thirdly, the establishment of inter-school curriculum working groups to pool experience and effort in pushing out the curriculum frontiers. Clearly, the intention was to create a balance between centralism and devolution.

Towards the end of 1987, four terms into the pilot, the Executive group (which comprises the heads of all the institutions involved, plus the Project Co-ordinator and members of the advisory service) asked the evaluators to look at 'some aspect of the management of the scheme', and it was suggested that the curriculum working groups would be a useful focus. Clearly this request was prompted by a degree of anxiety about the effectiveness of these groups. The research assistant therefore undertook a careful study, going through the minutes of every group and interviewing each school co-ordinator as well as the three curriculum leaders from the central team. Following that, the local team and the external consultant jointly produced a report on the issues which, in their judgement, emerged from the evidence, taking care to reflect the views that had been expressed by the people, concerned. In addition, an annex was added giving a detailed account of each group. The nub of the report was a page of questions which, it was suggested, 'needed to be addressed' if there were to be fruitful discussions about the future development of the working groups.

The rest of this paper summarises the issues raised and ends with the agenda of questions.

Setting up the Groups

Choosing the focus

Five of the curriculum working groups were set up at an early meeting of the TVEI project team. This group is made up of the scheme's co-ordinator, the curriculum leaders and the school co-ordinators and it has met weekly throughout the project. In retrospect, the members of the team felt that they would have benefited from a more careful consideration of the nature of the groups that were being set up.

The project team identified a large number of cross-curricula themes and chose two of them — Equal Opportunities and Profiling — as immediate priorities. In addition, subject specific groups in Business Studies, Home Economics and CDT were set up by the curriculum leaders on behalf of the project team. (The sixth group — the Design Education Cross-Curriculum group — was set up somewhat later as a result of an adviser-led and TRIST-supported initiative to explore the development of a modular CDT/HE course. It was convened by the curriculum leader for Technology.)

Organisational matters

When the groups were set up, the way in which they were to relate to the individual participating schools and to the TVEI managing groups had not been clarified and indeed some uncertainties about the interrelationships between the various groups and institutions persisted. One of the consequences of this lack of clarity was that groups were uncertain with whom they should negotiate their brief and to whom they should take their interim findings.

It was also unclear how TVEI curriculum development fitted into the overall pattern of curriculum development within the borough. For some groups, for example the Equal Opportunities group, questions of overlap and duplication were a concern. It was felt that, especially where the authority had a specialist adviser in the relevant area, closer links with the advisory team would have been helpful.

Curriculum working group meetings were not allocated directed time and a corollary of this was that representation was on the basis of self selection. In some instances schools were represented by individuals who had not been allocated a responsibility allowance for the area under consideration, either via the TVEI scheme or the school's normal points allowance. Some representatives had no clearly designated responsibility from their schools for curriculum development within the remit of the group they attended. One potential difficulty arising from this was the possibility of discrepancies between the views of 'representatives' and the policies of their schools. Only one third of group meetings were attended by representatives of all five schools and in some cases this, coupled with a lack of continuity in representation, meant that the composition of the group could change quite dramatically from one meeting to the next, with the obvious result that little progress could be made. Communications between the working groups and the individual schools became rather 'hit and miss' affairs as a result of the changes in representation and differences between the authority of representatives to speak for their schools.

Setting the brief

The groups decided on their own brief and the time constraints within which they expected to work. Members of the central team and the school co-ordinators were involved in this process but it does not appear that reference was made to the Executive group on which sit the headteachers of all the institutions involved in TVEI. It is unclear whether the TVEI steering groups within each school felt they had a role as sponsors of the curriculum working groups.

It seems therefore that the groups were set up without the sponsorship of senior management in the schools and without the purpose and possible consequences of their work having been clearly defined and recognised. The consequences of this were twofold: in the first place, the lack of sponsorship for the curriculum working groups resulted in teachers feeling that they had been let down when their hard work within the groups was not subsequently reflected in the curriculum of their schools; and secondly, the lack of consensus between participating schools as to the purpose of some groups led to tensions between them when it appeared that curriculum proposals developed in the group were in conflict with development within individual schools.

Variations in the Tasks Undertaken

Clearly the groups working within the TVEI option subject boundaries, Home Economics, CDT and Business Studies, spoke to a well defined recipient group. The intended outcomes of their work were new curriculum materials and the development of links with INSET. These groups were able to identify a specific task with clearly defined time limits which addressed a shared need. Although it was not formally stated, they had a clear dissemination strategy, i.e. that all the participants should benefit from shared effort.

Though working within the 'World of Technology', the Design Education Cross-Curriculum (DECC) group addressed its efforts across subject boundaries and faced the additional problem of working towards the goal of a common CDT/HE course at the same time as developments were moving these individual areas forward. Moreover, it was hard to identify a commonly perceived need between the five schools.

The work of the Equal Opportunities and Profiling groups had potential implications for a much wider audience. Their work was not focused by the same time constraints as the single subject groups. In addition, for these cross curricular areas the five schools had very different starting points. Both groups initiated a variety of tasks of their own choosing but found it difficult to identify a clear dissemination strategy.

Thus, given the very different nature of the tasks undertaken and the different audiences which they addressed, it is not surprising that the different groups had differing degrees of impact on curriculum development in schools.

Impact on School Practice

It is evident that the Business Education and the Home Economics groups have made a useful contribution to developing these areas of the curriculum. The school co-ordinators attributed their success to the fact that both groups had had the task of writing modules and assignments for new 100% coursework-assessed GCSE courses. The need to deliver materials had thus helped to focus the efforts of the group members and 'inspire people to work effectively'.

The CDT group did not achieve the same success as these two other groups. In the view of the curriculum leader the difference between the new GCSE courses and the courses previously offered was similar in scale to the difference between the old and the new Home Economics courses. However the view from the schools was that the group was starting from a 'base-line of existing courses'. It seems therefore that the work of this group was not focused by a collectively held perception of need. The extreme pressure on staffing in CDT departments was felt to have contributed to the problem of securing regular representation at the meetings of this group.

It was much more difficult for school co-ordinators to identify the specific contributions of the cross-curricular groups, Equal Opportunities and Profiling, although variations in their perceptions of impact may relate to differences in the starting points of the schools. In several cases the direction towards which the group had decided to direct its efforts did not reflect the concerns of the individual school. Where co-ordinators did identify developments in these areas, they attributed these not only to the work of the curriculum group but also to other factors, including the training provided by the central team and also to a pervasive sense within the school system of a need for change in these areas. The direct benefits of the group meetings were felt to be individual staff development which reinforced developmental work in some schools.

For some school co-ordinators it was particularly disappointing that no joint CDT/HE course had resulted from the work of the DECC group as they felt that, in their schools, the introduction of new courses within the World of Technology had been put on ice pending the outcome of the DECC initiative: they therefore felt doubly let down.

The Role of the Central Support Team

Clearly overall responsibility for leading and maintaining the direction of curriculum development rests with the Project Co-ordinator and inevitably the changes in personnel that have already been referred to led to some loss of continuity. However, the heavy administrative load of the Co-ordinator was a constraint noted both by the school co-ordinators in this study and in the NFER report on *The Management of TVEI* (Stoney *et al.*, 1986). In the first eighteen months of the scheme, only one curriculum working group meeting was attended by the Project Co-ordinator.

The curriculum leaders were, however, very much involved in the work of the groups. Five of the six groups were chaired by a curriculum leader, and the Equal Opportunities group was chaired by a school co-ordinator in conjunction with a curriculum leader. In this way good links with both INSET needs identification and course provision were made. Most of the school co-ordinators saw the curriculum leaders as having prime responsibility for the groups though at the same time they acknowledged the importance of drawing on the expertise of all group members. The general feeling that emerged was that where good relationships were established with the central team and there was visible support for the project in schools, teachers were more likely to give a high priority to the working groups.

There were, however, several factors which made it difficult for the curriculum leaders themselves to discern the precise role of the groups, and their own position within them. The root of some of these difficulties lay in the uncertainty about the degree to which the project was in fact centralised or devolved and the difficulty, noted in other TVEI evaluations, of centrally appointed staff establishing a role for themselves *vis à vis* the schools (Stoney *et al.*, 1986). The relationship was made more uneasy by a lack of consensus about the curriculum leader's role and the very exposed position in which they found themselves.

The Role of the School Steering Groups

The composition of the school steering group varied between the five schools and their concern to receive and communicate information to and from the working groups differed. Schools had not felt it necessary to address the question of how far their practice could or should be influenced by the deliberations of the curriculum working groups, and indeed the whole issue of the inter-relationships between them was unclear. The school co-ordinators also identified the need for improved communications within the schools, and this was seen as the shared responsibility of both themselves and senior management.

What's in it for Teachers?

The question of the 'rewards' for teachers attending group meetings, many of whom were not in receipt of a TVEI allowance and were attending in their own time, was felt to be an important consideration. All the school co-ordinators were concerned that the teachers involved should be able to come away from the meetings with something that would be of direct help to them in the classroom and which they could clearly identify as curriculum development. However, it is obviously more difficult to provide this kind of tangible benefit to teachers attending groups which aim to bring about a broader type of curriculum change.

There appears to be a relationship between individual professional development and curriculum development in that the integration of both elements seemed to re-inforce the work of the group. However, it is not only curriculum working group meetings which offer this opportunity. Meetings focusing primarily on teacher INSET might also be seen as valuable in terms of curriculum development by providing an occasion for the exchange of views and the sharing of expertise. There was some suggestion that where other initiatives were running in parallel (for example, CDT teachers in the authority were being offered INSET through the British Schools Technology scheme), one might develop at the expense of the other unless the relationship between them was clearly understood and seen as complementary.

Inter-school Curriculum Working Groups: Emerging Issues

In common with TVEI schemes nationally, it is evident that this TVEI programme has promoted greater inter-school liaison than had previously been the case. One way in which this has been brought about is by the formation and maintenance of the six curriculum working groups, some aspects of whose work have been examined in this study. The value of a collective approach to curriculum development work is emphasised in a national evaluation report (Harrison *et al.*, 1987) : however, the same report makes it clear that collaboration needs careful management if it is to achieve effective change.

The establishment of curriculum working groups has been a key part of the strategy for curriculum development in this scheme and the main way in which a collective and collaborative way working has been explored. Some notable successes have been recorded, but in considering the work of the groups to date, a number of issues have emerged. The questions below were drawn from the evidence presented above, and were presented by the evaluators to the Executive group with the suggestion that they needed to be addressed if the strategy for collaborative curriculum development is to be strengthened in the second half of the pilot scheme. It is also possible that they may be of more general use within the authority when similar initiatives are planned.

1. What are the links between TVEI curriculum development and other curriculum development initiatives within the authority?
2. How might the question of the extent to which the TVEI scheme is centralised or devolved be resolved in relation to specific issues?
3. What is the purpose of the group? Is it a group with a short term specific task or a group working towards a wider type of curriculum change? What implications does the nature of the task have for the way in which the group works?
4. Who has the responsibility for negotiating the brief, locating the group within the management structure, and considering its reports?
5. Is the purpose of the group endorsed by senior management within the participating institutions and to what extent do they have a commitment to the outcomes?
6. To what extent are the group members representatives of their institutions? To what extent is recognition given for attendance?
7. How might effective communications between group and institutions be established and maintained?

Conclusion and Postscript by the External Consultant

This study is interesting, and quite possibly useful outside the authority and outside TVEI. The capacity of teachers to work productively together in co-operative groups is, and will continue to be, a testing ground for teacher professionalism: put bluntly, if we can't do it, we may deserve to have every detail of teaching programmes arrive in an envelope from the DES. But this chapter implies that if such groups are to be productive, certain conditions are helpful and certain others are inhibiting. LEAs and schools can get them right — or they can get them wrong. The groups discussed in this chapter were set up in the spirit of TVEI: 'to explore and test new ways of managing and organising the curriculum . . .'. The authority is now taking steps to review how such groups will be set up and supported in the future and this is the kind of response that evaluators hope for. Moreover, now the question has been raised, the project has begun to look at the issue of centralisation versus devolution. The evaluation has therefore helped to build a framework for this process of looking at past experience and reflecting upon future action, not least in relation to difficult questions about where initiative, decision making and responsibility should lie in relation to a given issue. In a sense, it may be that curriculum working groups (by that, or many other names) are used within education generally to put off, or even obscure, delicate questions of this kind: this study suggests that without clear thinking about such matters, cross-institutional groups have a very difficult role.

And finally, the post-script. This chapter was prepared for an evaluators' conference and therefore it may not be amiss to comment on the role of evaluation as it is conceived within this study. The intention was to produce a piece of genuinely useful evaluation and thereby to assert the value of formative work. I trust that it does its bit to demonstrate that evaluation is about more than monitoring, more than policing the achievement of specific objectives, and more than enforcing accountability through the pursuit of performance indicators. Useful evaluation is future-orientated and in a sense is only concerned with the past as a way of making experience available to future decision making. I would hope that this study will help the authority to experiment further with cross-institutional working groups; and to do it all the better for having an embryonic map based on the first two years' safari.

References

Harrison, M. *et al.* 1987, *The TVEI Curriculum 14–16: A Summary.* London: MSC/Training Agency.

Stoney, S. M. *et al.* 1986, *The Management of TVEI: A Summary.* London: MSC/Training Agency.

5 The problem of teaching style in TVEI

MARTIN MERSON
Department of Education, University of Warwick

The problem of teaching style is a complex and sensitive one since it goes to the heart of matters such as teacher competence and effectiveness. The problem is all the more sensitive in the climate of teacher criticism which has prevailed in Britain since the mid-1970s. Teaching styles cannot be divorced from the debate about the standards of achievement of pupils or the relevance of the curriculum to the economic needs of society.

It is into the context of this debate that the Manpower Services Commission intruded its own model of good practice within the aims of TVEI such that:

> they (the pupils) become accustomed to using their skills and knowledge to solve real world problems they will meet at work; more emphasis is placed on developing initiative, motivation and enterprise as well as problem solving skills and other aspects of personal development.
> (MSC, 1983)

Nothing is said directly about the teaching styles but by implication they must be the kinds of styles which encourage the above activities.

Regardless of the commonsense ring about the MSC aims, the issue of teaching style seems vulnerable from two vantage points; there is the view that progressive and informal teaching styles were in part responsible for the claimed decline in standards in the 1970s; there is the opposing view that teachers adopt traditional and directive styles of teaching which do not encourage the learning which society values. The debate is somewhat more complicated by lack of shared meaning as to what constitutes traditional and progressive styles of teaching, and indeed the lack of any hard evidence as to the relative prevalence of such styles or the effectiveness of them. This enables the DES and indeed HMI to take inconsistent positions on the issue from time to time. The DES (1977) in its important consultative paper *Education in Schools* when describing child-centred methods, suggests:

> It (child-centred methods) has proved to be a trap for some less able or less experienced teachers who applied the freer methods uncritically or failed to recognise that they require careful planning of the opportunities offered to children and the systematic monitoring of the progress of individuals . . . In some classes, or even some schools, the use of the child-centred approach has deteriorated into lack of order and application.
> (DES, 1977; para 2.29)

The above quotation refers to primary practice, but primary schools are continually held up as models of good pedagogical practice for secondary teachers. In 1979, HMI published their lament about the dominance of poor formal methods in the last two years of secondary schools and in effect present a contrary view to the DES:

> Another question is whether the styles of teaching and learning which are widely employed are necessarily conducive to the best examination results or the best education. Such styles typically included heavily directed teaching, a preponderance of dictated or copied notes, an emphasis on the giving or recall of information, with little room or time for enquiry or exploration of applications.
> (DES (HMI), 1979: para 10, page 262)

This 'evidence' was based on the survey of 10% of secondary schools in England and Wales, conducted during 1977/78. If this seems somewhat dated, the more recent document *Secondary Schools: An Appraisal by HMI* (DES, 1988) suggests little has changed:

> Many lessons indicated that for the majority of pupils learning and teaching, in terms both of pace, content and approach, have changed little since 1979. Pupils continue to spend a large amount of their time in classrooms listening or writing; in later years of schools the total volume of their written work was usually considerable.
> (DES (HMI), 1988: para 60, page 16)

It may be considered unfair to select views from DES and HMI which compare unfavourable accounts of progressivism at primary level, with unfavourable accounts of traditionalism at secondary level, and yet the teacher finds him/herself caught between such images and might be tempted to find some middle way. There is also the question of to what extent such 'offical' views can be considered as sound evidence of how teachers *are* teaching and indeed how they *ought* to be teaching. One might be encouraged to imagine how teachers teach when being 'inspected', certainly one would sympathise with those teachers who exhibit a reluctance to take risks in front of HMI. It might be entirely possible that HMI are presented with a rather conservative sample of practice on their rounds. This might go some way to explaining the very surprising claim presented in their survey of primary schools in England, (DES (HMI), 1978), that:

> In the survey classes about three quarters of teachers employed a mainly didactic approach, while less than one in twenty relied mainly on an exploratory approach. In about one-fifth of the classes teachers employed an appropriate combination of didactic and exploratory methods, varying their approach according to the nature of the task in hand . . .
> (para 3.20, page 27)

The debate about teaching styles then is very much of a hortatory nature with little recourse to evidence, apart from HMI surveys, and little in the way of explicit justification or theory certainly as far as the MSC and FEU (another zealous contributor to the debate) are concerned. There is however, an extensive literature of theories and investigations into teaching styles well summarised by Anthony (1979). It is hard to estimate to what extent teachers will have been influenced, however partially, by sources of research evidence and theory, again mostly focused at primary level. Doubtless there is a drift of findings such as those of Bennett (1976), which for all the criticism of sample and statistical methods, presented a view not sympathetic to progressive methods, and a view which will have influenced the climate of ideas. However, perhaps it is not the findings themselves which are most valuable but the questions raised, some of which can be usefully translated to the context of TVEI. The ORACLE study, Galton & Simon (1980), is a case in point, not again for any tentative results as to the efficacy of particular styles for particular purposes or for particular kinds of pupils, but because the study raised some interesting issues as to how teachers actually teach.

The ORACLE study uses a *close scrutiny* of teaching processes; the types of questions, task statements and routine statements made to pupils, whether they are open or closed, whether they are related to intellectual tasks or simple organisational tasks in the room; how children are grouped and so on. Teachers were seen to use a complex and *varied range of styles* and were grouped by the predominance of their mode of interaction with pupils. Four broad categories of teacher style were found: individual monitors; class enquirers; group instructors; style changers (these were further sub-divided into three groups).

From the ORACLE study a number of considerations emerge:

a) teachers adopt a range of styles;
b) close observation of teacher-pupil interaction is required for very broad classification of style;
c) of interest is the appropriateness of teaching-style to the particular task;
d) impression gained from ORACLE is that teachers have access to a range of styles but choose to adopt a particular range or pattern of styles for *particular reasons*;
e) there is also the issue of appropriateness of teaching style to type of pupil.

To these considerations a further avenue beyond the strict preoccupations of the ORACLE study suggests itself, and that is the appropriateness of the style(s) adopted to characteristics of the teacher, e.g. teacher confidence and expertise.

The above considerations reveal some of the confusion of official images of 'good teaching style' provided by the DES and HMI. There are also the many pessimistic empirical studies as to the efficacy of progressive styles, such as Bennett's, which find their way, in an attenuated form, to influence the teacher's consciousness. Taken together these are the messages about 'how to teach' which will compete with the models enshrined in the TVEI aims.

It was against this background that the evaluation of teaching styles was conducted in the TVEI pilot projects in two authorities in the West Midlands. The ORACLE study oriented the evaluation towards preoccupations such as complexity of styles and the notion of appropriateness of style to task and pupil type. Thus of interest to the evaluator was, firstly, the *nature* of the style or styles adopted by teachers within TVEI activities and, secondly, the reasons for the adoption of particular styles. *Reasons* were classified as pedagogical, practical and professional. The pedagogic included congruence with the teacher's beliefs about teaching and learning, appropriateness to type of pupil and appropriateness to task; the practical included the influence of class size and levels of equipment; professional considered the teacher's view of his/her own ability to adopt particular styles effectively. Evaluation was conducted by observation and conversation and the sample was limited by the costs of such 'labour intensive' work against the resources available for evaluation.

Thirty-one teachers were observed in 12 schools across two metropolitan authorities. About 1.5 hours were spent observing each teacher in the classroom and a further one hour in conversation with the teacher and, in some cases, with pupils. Conversation was also used to try and establish how representative the observed lesson was of the teacher's repertoire of teaching styles and hence avoid the snapshot effect. The subjects observed were: technology; applied science; graphic and commercial art; business studies; media studies. All groups were in the fifth year, the last year of compulsory education.

The framework used to interpret the teaching styles was a simple twofold classification adopted from the HMI Primary Survey (DES (HMI), 1978), that of the exploratory and the didactic. This classification was used initially by HMI for observation of primary teaching and yet appealed to the evaluator as having features which made it appropriate to the context of TVEI. The classification was used to recognise the predominance of any style or any pattern of styles.

> A didactic style was one in which the teacher directed the childrens' work in accordance with relatively specific and predetermined intentions and where explanations usually, though not always, preceded the action taken by children.
>
> An exploratory approach was one in which the broad objectives of the work were discussed with the children but where they were then put in a position of finding their own solutions to the problems posed and of making choices about the way in which work was to be tackled. The scope and timescale of the tasks involved were likely to be flexible and the path of work was likely to be modified in the light of events; explanation by the teacher more often accompanied or followed action taken by the children.
> (para 3.19)

The exploratory style has features which are highly congruent with the aims of TVEI, such as the encouragement of initiative and problem solving.

Findings and Issues

Out of the 31 teachers observed, 29 used predominantly the exploratory form of teaching while being observed. One of the two teachers, who adopted a predominantly didactic style, invited the evaluator to observe another lesson in a subject 'in which she felt more confident' and presented a predominantly exploratory lesson. Most of the work observed was of a 'project' nature, pupils were individually, or in small groups, engaged in pursuing a task, usually one in which they had some element of choice. This was true of technology, graphic and commercial art and media studies, it was less true of business studies where the projects or tasks were often of a realistic but rather routine nature.

In technology, the projects consisted of examples such as developing a fish-bite detector, an automatic curtain control for the disabled and a pencil sharpener for the disabled. Each project had planning, construction and reviewing phases. In graphic and commercial art, projects involved designing and producing a book cover, a record sleeve and the cover for a contemporary magazine. Across the subject boundaries, all project work rested on a sound basis of skill development and an understanding of fairly sophisticated conceptual frameworks. In one example of business studies, the activities were selected to mirror as closely as possible the tasks encountered in a real office context. There were some 40 tasks involving correspondence, estimates and simple strategies in somewhat fragmented isolation which seemed, however 'realistic', somewhat dull and undemanding to a wide range of the pupils. It might be observed in passing that the principle of realism so fundamental to the 'philosophy' of TVEI, is not always able to motivate worthwhile learning.

During conversation with the evaluator the majority of the teachers also claimed to use a didactic style for particular purposes and at particular stages in their courses. Both technology and applied science teachers referred to regular pulses of didactic work, described as 'chalk and talk' to get certain basic ideas across. The media teachers referred to didactic occasions such as introduction to how to use the dark room or how to use the chemicals in photographic development. The picture that emerged was that the majority of teachers used both styles from time to time for pedagogic reasons and that the styles were used in a pattern or sequence determined by subject matter and tasks. With some teachers, such as graphic and commercial art teachers, the courses seemed to be front-loaded with didactic emphasis perhaps for the acquisition of basic skills; often this process took a long time, as much as a whole term. With technology teachers the didactic was regular and phased. When talking with pupils, two broad responses were encountered. High ability pupils (as classified by the school) seemed tolerant of all the teaching styles they experienced. Low ability pupils expressed low tolerance for either long periods of didactic teaching and, contrary to expectations, low tolerance of long periods of exploratory teaching, since 'they got bored and tended to mess around'.

What then can be distilled from the above observations and discussion? It would appear that the majority of teachers in this sample in the context of TVEI adopt a range of teaching styles for which they have pedagogical justifications. Such justifications relate mainly to the type of task which they are engaged upon. The didactic seems to be adopted for the transmission of basic skills or simple information. The exploratory style seems to be used with certain kinds of project work.

A very small minority of teachers appeared insecure in the adoption of exploratory teaching styles and this was explained by them in terms of their lack of confidence in the subject matter. This raises the wider concern of the match of teachers, in terms of their qualifications and experience, to the subjects they are expected to teach. Is it the case that teachers in general who are required to operate in subject areas where they have limited background and experience, tend to be less adventurous in their teaching strategies? If this is so, we might expect a greater strain to be experienced by teachers in TVEI than elsewhere given that the very subject areas of TVEI are amongst those most difficult to staff, an observation made by HMI in their first report on TVEI (DES (HMI), 1985b).

There is room for further investigation of the appropriateness of teaching styles and patterns of such styles to the needs of different types of pupils. Under consideration here are questions of the length of the episode of various teaching styles and the relationship between the episodes. Also the tolerance of particular types of pupils to such episodes and crude ability might not be the only classification of pupil need. Contrary to its earlier position, the DES has recently taken a more catholic view on teaching styles, although it is doubtful how long such a view will be maintained. In the White Paper *Better Schools* (DES, 1985a) it is suggested that:

> Every teacher needs a repertoire of teaching styles. At times, for example, every teacher properly adopts the traditional expert authority role, providing information, explanation and opinion. At other times, teachers need to guide learning less formally, promoting individual and group enquiry, and sharing discovery with the pupils. Teaching styles have to be varied sensitively to match the nature of the work in hand and the characteristics of the pupils as well as their stage of development.
> (para 134, page 41)

Some recognition must be made of the resource context of the above study since this will have implications for how generalisable any observations can be. In one authority the class size observed was between 7 and 15, and in the other between 10 and 17. The standard of equipment and its availability were well beyond that normally encountered in the mainstream of secondary work. Such factors greatly facilitate the opportunity for teachers to encourage investigatory and practical work and to engage in the supervision of individual pupils and groups at work. It remains to be argued whether teachers with more traditional sized groups of 25+ with access to a more modest array of equipment would consider a different pattern of teaching. Also any serious consideration of teaching style surely assumes recruitment of teachers with appropriate expertise and confidence in their subject area and in the wider matters relating to pedagogy. An assumption which in the light of current government policy cannot be taken for granted in many of the TVEI subject areas.

References

ANTHONY, W. 1979, Progressive learning theories: The evidence. In G. BERNBAUM (ed.), *Schooling in Decline*. London: MacMillan.

BENNETT, N. 1976, *Teaching Styles and Pupil Progress*. London: Open Books.

DES 1977, *Education in Schools: A Consultative Document*. London: HMSO.

— (HMI) 1978, *Primary Education in England: A Survey by HM Inspectors of Schools*. London: HMSO.

— (HMI) 1979, *Aspects of Secondary Education in England: A Survey by HM Inspectors of Schools*. London: HMSO.

— 1985a, *Better Schools* (CMND 9469). London: HMSO.

— (HMI) 1985b, *The Technical and Vocational Education Initiative: Early Developments: A Report by HM Inspectors*. London: HMSO.

— (HMI) 1988, *Secondary Schools: An Appraisal by HMI*. London: HMSO.

GALTON, M. and SIMON, B. 1980, *Progress and Performance in the Primary Classroom*. London: Routledge and Kegan Paul.

MSC 1983, *Aims of the Technical and Vocational Education Initiative*.

6 Evaluating teaching and learning styles in TVEI

GILL DAVIDSON and CARL PARSONS
The Evaluation Unit,
Christ Church College,
Canterbury

Introduction

With the advent of Extension one of the most pertinent issues in the management of TVEI is the permeation of 'new teaching and learning styles', as this to a large extent is the essence of TVEI. Understandably this has become an important focus for evaluation with projects anxious to identify just what teaching styles have been adopted in TVEI and the problems and issues related to their extension across the curriculum.

This chapter is in three parts. It examines the (lack of agreed) criteria for TVEI teaching and learning styles and then describes the methodology and findings of a study across two TVEI pilot projects. The chapter concludes with problems associated with reporting an evaluation which takes as its focus something as sensitive as teacher classroom practice and the difficulties faced by teachers in responding constructively to an evaluation report dealing with their practice.

This chapter arises from recent experience of evaluating teaching and learning styles in two TVEI pilot schemes but the problems and issues raised are, in our experience, more generally applicable.

Classroom observation is, by its very nature, expensive of evaluators' time and thus any local evaluation is necessarily selective both in terms of the range and number of lessons observed and in the range of focuses within the observation. The purpose of the evaluation can only be to raise issues which may form the basis for discussion or further investigation by teachers and other protaganists and stakeholders. The sensitive nature of classroom observation necessitates great diplomacy in consultations with schools over the brief, in negotiating access to classrooms and in maintaining relationships through and at the conclusion to the observation. Greater care is needed in evaluations with this focus to preserve anonymity or to agree release where the context and events described reveal an identity. There is a need for considerable delicacy and knowledge of audience when reporting whether it be feedback to the individual teachers, a school or a TVEI project steering group.

Defining Criteria

The pedagogical expectations of TVEI have not been made explicit in the national or indeed local guidelines and can only be inferred from key phrases and statements contained within the original aims and criteria. For instance a shift of emphasis from the content to the process of learning is implied by statements such as 'a curriculum that will develop skills and interests', particularly 'problem solving skills'. The content is constrained by the necessity for what is learnt to be 'of direct value to them at work' and 'knowledge with a more direct appreciation of the practical application'. As well as the focus upon personal and social skills, for instance, 'more emphasis is placed on developing initiative motivation and enterprise' and a curriculum appropriate to 'students' individual needs'. TVEI has subsequently championed such approaches as 'student centred learning', 'active learning', 'experiential learning', 'self directed study', and these phrases are bandied around as if their meaning were self evident and the value of such approaches to teaching undeniable. In reality the criteria to identify these teaching styles are rarely made clear and there is a danger in TVEI that there is a shared vocabulary but not necessarily shared meanings. After all, what opportunity does the average teacher have to observe other colleagues or engage in discussion about teaching style? There are as yet few mechanisms to identify and disseminate 'good practice'. Indeed many teachers may find themselves confused by the rhetoric and uncertain how to proceed. Whilst there are many claims made for the value of student centred or active learning, particularly with regard to self empowerment of the learner, there is little, if any, research evidence to back up these assertions. Despite this teachers find themselves under pressure to adopt 'new styles of teaching' without having a clear idea of what they are or being convinced by their value.

The recent volume in the National Evaluation from the University of Leeds (Barnes *et al.*, 1987) identified three styles of teaching — controlled, framed, negotiated — along a continuum related to the degree of participation and attempted to provide criteria (see Table 6.1) related to each style.

TABLE 6.1 *The participation dimension*

	CONTROLLED	*FRAMED*	*NEGOTIATED*
Content	Tightly controlled by teacher. Not negotiable.	Teacher controls topic, frames of reference and tasks; criteria explicit.	Discussed at each point; joint decisions. made
Focus	Authoritative knowledge and skills; simplified, monolithic.	Stress on empirical testing; processes chosen by teacher; some legitimation of student ideas.	Search for justifications and principles; strong legitimation of student ideas.
Students' Role	Acceptance; routine performance; little access to principles.	Join in teacher's thinking; make hypotheses, set up tests; operate teacher's frame.	Discuss goals and methods critically; share responsibility for frame and criteria.
Key Concepts	'Authority': the proper procedures and the right answers.	'Access': to skills, processes, criteria.	'Relevance': critical discussion of students' priorities.
Methods	Exposition; worksheets (closed); note-giving; individual exercises; routine practical work. Teacher evaluates.	Exposition, with discussion eliciting suggestions; indiv./group problem-solving; lists of tasks given; discussion of outcomes, but teacher adjudicates.	Group and class discussion and decision-making about goals and criteria. Students plan and carry out work, make presentations, evaluate success.

By and large TVEI is thought to reflect the right side of the continuum characterised by pupil participation, responsibility and a variety of skills. However, much of the teaching they actually observed in TVEI lessons was described as controlled or framed.

There are other schemes representing similar continua; Bartlett & Cox (1982) propose a continuum of pupil learning activities with four categories — reception learning, problem solving and hypothesis testing, open ended discovery, and creative activity; the right of the continuum representing increased pupil autonomy and a diminishing of teacher involvement. A recent TRIST paper (MSC, 1988) proposes four teaching approaches, didactic, guiding, collaborating and enabling. They suggest that if personal and social objectives are to be realised these cannot be delivered didactically and require 'active learning',

> . . . as the only way of delivering certain objectives and therefore as part of an entitlement curriculum.

Although not denying a role for the didactic where information and knowledge are uppermost they present 20 criteria for 'active learning', for example,

- — Activities carried out by pupils are variable and negotiated with the teacher;
- — Pupil activities are mainly problem solving and experimental;
- — The main activity of the teacher is to facilitate and enable pupils to learn.

However, all the continua of teaching and learning styles we have examined actually present problems when one tries to communicate to diverse audiences. The report of the Leeds National Evaluation team is evocative and has achieved the status 'of a good read'. The audience for their report has been general and dispersed and there has not been the expectation that specific identifiable groups will react to the implications of the report. Local evaluations do have specific local groups in mind who might be expected to respond to the report by trying to develop their teaching to a point where it more closely approximates to the model of 'TVEI teaching and learning styles.'

With all continua of social interaction there are no clear or precise boundaries between categories and no matter how well trained the researchers there are no means to ensure that perceptions of the boundaries will be consistent between researchers or even for the same researcher over a period of time. Criteria one might apply are ambiguous by their nature, and, unless prescribed technical meanings, are subject to cultural and personal interpretation.

The notion of teaching style is multifaceted; it covers roles, relationships, authority, participation and control over time, content, movement, activity, assessment and relevance. Teachers or other implicated parties may accentuate one or several of these features or weight them in idiosyncratic combinations.

The lack of clear and shared criteria for understanding and interpreting classroom behaviour poses problems for evaluation particularly in the communication of findings to teachers. It is even more problematic if such observations are committed to paper. The issue of reporting will be further developed but it highlights the necessity for various levels of dialogue in the evaluation process.

Methodology

A total of 79 lessons was observed in seven schools across two local authorities. The lessons were varied across all the TVEI options and also included a number of non-TVEI subjects. In one of the LEAs, in an attempt to alleviate the tendency toward the general, it was decided to focus on three of the schools participating in the project with the aim of providing specific feedback to teachers and schools directly involved, as well as an overview of general issues and problems arising from the whole investigation which would be of relevance to all of the institutions in the consortium.

In each of the schools a TVEI pupil was shadowed for a day by an evaluator, visiting TVEI and non-TVEI lessons in order to sample the range of activities a pupil might be engaged in and to gain a perspective on the teaching strategies employed outside TVEI. This activity also helped to give a clearer impression of the school ethos, general expectations and relationships.

The variation of classroom activity one might encounter necessitates a flexible methodology. The evaluators were equipped with an observation schedule designed to record classroom activities (See Figure 6.1.). Recordings were taken at five minute intervals during lessons of:

a) the type of activity students were engaged in;
b) the type of working unit;
c) whether the activity was teacher directed, framed by the teacher with some freedom within it for students to initiate ideas, or student directed.

Where possible the degree of interaction between teachers and pupils was noted by recording the occasions when teachers spoke to pupils and vice

DATE .... SUBJECT .... CLASS SIZE GIRLS ...... BOYS ...... OBSERVER ....
TIME .... TEACHER ....

CODES.

WRITING
1. Copying/Dictation
2. Notemaking/Writing Up
3. Creative/Individual
4. Graphics/Diagrams
5. Design/Planning/Solving

WATCHING
1. Demonstration
2. Video/film
3. Slides/film strip

WORKING UNIT
1. Individual
2. Pair
3. Group
4. Class

STUDENT/TEACHER LED
1. Teacher Directed
2. Framed/Negotiated
3. Student Directed

ACTIVITY / Time (mins)	5	10	15	20	25	30	35	40	45	50	55	60	65	70	75	80	85	90	95	100
Talking to teacher																				
Talking to pupils																				
Listening to teacher																				
Listening to pupils																				
Reading																				
Writing																				
Doing/Making																				
Watching																				
Thinking																				
No organised activity																				
Working unit																				
Student/teacher led																				

THREATS/ADMONISHMENTS
Boy
Girl
Class

TEACHER PUPIL INTERACTION
Boy
Girl

USE OF NAMES
Boys
Girls

TEACHER/CONTACT

	Student Initiated	Teacher Initiated
Instantaneous		
Up to 1/2 minute		
1/2 to 1 minute		
over 1 minute		

FIGURE 6.1 *Classroom observation record*

versa. In some lessons the use of student names was also recorded. The observation schedule was not always appropriate, designed as schedules are for lessons where it is assumed that at any one time pupils are engaged in the same or similar activities.

Much of the information was collected through field notes which were guided by a set of questions (Figure 6.2) under three headings, the physical environment, the social human environment, and teaching and learning activities. Where possible, aspects of the lesson and classroom processes were discussed with teachers and pupils.

Findings

Classroom data of this kind are by their nature very complex and analysis is made more difficult by the lack of clear and shared criteria. In the analysis the assumption was made that 'TVEI teaching and learning styles' should reflect a 'negotiated' (Barnes *et al.*, 1987) or 'active learning' style and that pupil involvement and control of content and procedures was to be valued. Using the questions (see Figure 6.2) as a framework we were able to make comparisons of classroom processes within the data set and to consider the relative degree of variation between the lessons we had observed. While each lesson could be described in detail and contained a wealth of information what follows is a brief outline of some of the salient findings and issues which arose from the study as a whole and which have general applicability. In this section we have particularly tried to highlight some of the difficulties and contradictions we observed in relation to criteria for 'negotiated' or 'active' approaches to teaching and learning.

Physical environment

Lessons were observed in a variety of physical settings including traditional classrooms, specially designed classrooms, laboratories, workshops, a gymnasium and so forth; these were suitable to the task to a greater or lesser extent. However, it is true that many TVEI teachers have made great efforts to improve the quality of the teaching environment despite not being placed in appropriate physical settings.

Physical Environment

1. What is the physical layout of the classroom. Does it change according to the nature of the activities? How flexible is the working environment?
2. Is there freedom of movement around the classroom? Who controls classroom spaces? What territories are occupied by pupils and teachers?

Social Human Environment

1. What interactions take place between teacher and pupils and pupils and pupils?
2. What forms of address are used? Does the teacher know and use pupil names?
3. Are pupils allowed to speak spontaneously?
4. How is classroom discipline maintained? Does the teacher threaten or punish?
5. Are boys and girls treated equally?
6. How are decisions made in the classroom? What degree of negotiation takes place?

Teaching and Learning Activities

1. How is the lesson presented? Are the aims, context, purpose, made clear? Are these shared?
2. What activities do pupils engage in during the lesson?
3. Are the pupils engaged in choice? Who controls the learning activities? How much legitimation of pupil ideas?
4. Is the time spent on activities flexible or fixed?
5. What is the role and activity of the teacher throughout the lesson?
6. Are the resources varied, sufficient and appropriate to the task? How are these used? Who controls them?
7. What is the content of the lesson? Is it related to pupil experience or interest? What are the contexts in which it can be applied? Are these made clear?
8. Is there any attempt to relate or refer to the wider community?
9. What are the learning outcomes?
10. Is there any attempt to evaluate the lesson? By whom?

FIGURE 6.2 *TVEI teaching and learning styles aide memoire*

It is clear from our observations that the physical environment can impinge greatly on the learning process and particularly affect the social and human environment of the classroom. On the whole insufficient attention was given to seating arrangements in classrooms and these often form a barrier to communications and affect group cohesion. The physical layout of furniture can be incongruent with the social human atmosphere teachers claim to be trying to create. Although in some cases the furniture in classrooms inhibited possibilities for rearrangement there were often simple changes which could have been made to enhance group cohesion and improve social atmosphere.

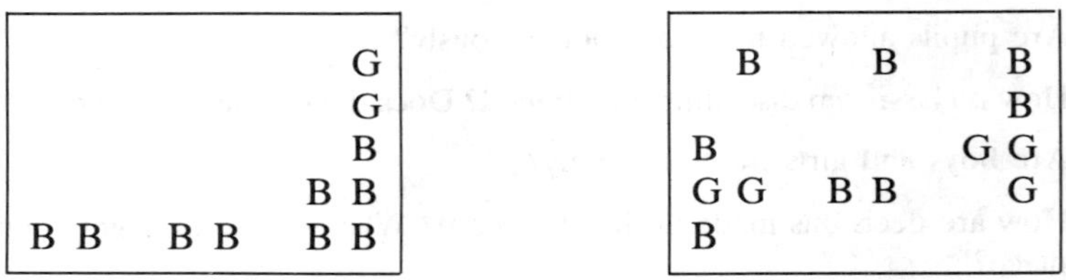

B=boy
G=girl

FIGURE 6.3 *Example of seating arrangements in TVEI classes*

The two examples in Figure 6.3, both lessons of class discussion, illustrate the lack of cohesion in the group as well as the separation of the gender groups. There is possibly a case for teachers to impose certain seating arrangements in the short term to overcome some of these problems despite the obvious impingement of pupil choice.

Pupils seem to appreciate 'freedom of movement' in the classrooms and on the whole react positively to situations where they are free to control their own space. This happens most often in workshops. In a number of lessons pupils were constrained behind desks and teachers delivered things to them; pupil responsibility is undermined in these circumstances and clearly an important factor in affecting behaviour. Some TVEI classrooms have been purposefully designed into attractive working environments often carpeted with new furniture or fittings. In these circumstances pupils generally behave more responsibly and the atmosphere is akin to an adult working environment with a greater degree of mutual trust between teachers and pupils. Where teaching rooms have been purposefully designed a much greater flexibility can be introduced. A lack of flexibility in the physical environment can affect the possibilities for learning; this was particularly observed in PSE lessons.

It is interesting to speculate whether the physical environment imposes particular teaching styles to the extent that a changed environment could stimulate changes in approach. The TVEI Director of one of the projects had adopted the phrase 'the carpet led curriculum' in support of such a notion.

It is still true that in all of the schools the classroom layout with desks facing the front was the most common. This suggests a particular style of teaching and creates a dominant ethos of 'teacher authority' which is in conflict with the philosophy of TVEI and was clearly confusing for many teachers. There is a lot yet to be done to allay the messages of the 'hidden curriculum' in this context if TVEI teaching and learning style is to be spread across the curriculum.

Social human environment

In general in TVEI lessons in all of the schools there is a characteristic social style and atmosphere which is based on more informal relationships between pupils and teachers and freer interactions between the pupils themselves, the emphasis tending towards co-operation rather than competition. The degree of interaction that pupils have with the teacher and other pupils varies but on the whole is greatest in TVEI lessons and particularly when pupils are engaged in small group work. The less formal atmosphere of many TVEI lessons encourages spontaneity and therefore increases the level of participation of pupils. Formal forms of address and rituals such as raising hands are still most common and could be said to create an atmosphere of teacher authority. Some teachers seemed to be trying to adopt a more open style of teaching in that they released control over content but somewhat incongruously maintained an authoritarian stance over classroom discipline. In such an atmosphere pupils are unlikely to feel relaxed and treated as partners in the learning process. There seems to be a need to consider alternative ways of establishing classroom discipline by involving the pupils in establishing ground rules and procedures; this was rarely observed.

Although most teachers were committed to the need to avoid sex stereotyping and sexist behaviour there were some inconsistencies in the translation of intentions into practice. For instance, boys names are used far more than girls and boys receive much more attention from teachers. There are fewer gender interchanges in groups and boys and girls generally sit apart; often girls are marginalised by their choice of seating. There were some examples of stereotyping in reading materials and a number of teachers use gender specific language and reinforce sexist behaviour. If equal opportunity is to have meaning in TVEI there is still a need to further raise teachers' awareness of the difficult issues relating to gender in the light of observations made.

Teaching and learning activities

The majority of the teachers in TVEI had made significant changes in their teaching approaches and were genuinely striving to adopt a more open and negotiated style which allows for more freedom and legitimation of pupil ideas. However, the transition towards this style is not easy particularly as the vast majority of teaching in secondary schools is still largely didactic or controlled and in the schools observed the school ethos reflected this approach. There are many constraints upon teachers even where there is a strong commitment, and translation into practice is dependent upon a range of factors including the existing expertise and experience of teachers, the existing skills and expectations of the pupils, institutional ethos and organisation, resources and in-service training. There are clearly variations between schools in how teachers perceive their role and a wide variety of teaching strategies were observed. As the Leeds report acknowledges the scope for introducing negotiated styles of teaching varies considerably between subjects and also at different stages of a course and therefore it is difficult to say that there was any dominant or shared pedagogy in TVEI lessons. There were some obvious contrasts with non-TVEI lessons in that there were more opportunities for pupils to share ideas and work in small groups.

TABLE 6.2 *Variations of working unit and teacher directed activity*

	Non-TVEI	TVEI		Non-TVEI	TVEI
Individual	64%	9%	Teacher directed	100%	49%
Pair	3%	0%	Framed/Negotiated	0%	25%
Groups	0%	38%	Student Directed	0%	28%
Class	33%	53%			

Table 6.2 shows the variations of working unit and the degree to which the activities were directed by the teacher, in TVEI and non-TVEI lessons in one school. On the whole there was more freedom and responsibility allocated to the pupils and more opportunities for discussion and participation in TVEI than non-TVEI lessons. Pupils when interviewed generally preferred the TVEI lessons and felt they responded well and were appreciative when teachers 'treated them as adults'.

Whilst every individual lesson could be reported in detail and provide useful data, the following observations are general problems or issues which may be common to other TVEI projects.

The genuine 'negotiated' curriculum was rarely observed even where there were no examination constraints. Teachers nearly always defined the tasks and there was very little evidence of pupils negotiating the content and direction of a course. There was a degree of choice or freedom within activities to a greater or lesser extent but not between them. In subjects where pupils were engaged in project work such as CDT or Graphics there was the greatest freedom to take responsibility for their own work and more likelihood of negotiation taking place between teachers and pupils.

The reluctance of many teachers to give up their control of content was observed even in group discussion where the teacher played, perhaps unconsciously, a directive role. In such situations where a teacher is present the pupils direct their discussion through them; the role of the teacher as 'expert' is still very evident in most classrooms. There are cases of teachers choosing examples, afraid that pupils will not come up with anything. It may be that teachers feel that by losing control of the content or their authority over a subject they lose status. This is a very real threat in a particular school ethos which exacerbates such expectations of teachers. The degree of control over content exercised by the teachers depended to a large extent upon the emphasis on factual content. In programmes with specific knowledge objectives the outcomes are pre-defined which limits flexibility. Whereas some courses are clearly restricted by examinations, there were some non-examinable courses where teachers had made facts one of the main outcomes, so that there was perhaps some internal inconsistency between content and method. There is a very real question about the extent to which it is possible to combine objectives of factual knowledge with the student 'negotiated' style of teaching.

In lessons where there are objectives of factual knowledge the purpose may be obvious to pupils and they can feel they have learned something. In many active TVEI lessons this is much less obvious, the purpose of activities is not always made clear and some pupils interviewed were obviously having difficulty making sense of their experiences. Particularly in P.S.E. lessons the outcomes and purpose of activities are less obvious. Our observations support the view that on the whole teachers should spend more time contextualising activities and emphasise their explicit relevance. Much more effort could be made to transfer ownership of task and activities to the pupils and allow them more opportunity to relate them to their own priorities.

If pupils are genuinely to feel responsibility for their own learning then they must be involved in these two important phases, choosing and negotiating activities and evaluating outcomes. This is particularly pertinent if pupils are to be involved in assessment.

It is impossible here to consider in detail the variation of the activities pupils were engaged in, and the degree to which they were problem solving and experimenting varied greatly between lessons. Some subjects obviously lend themselves much more easily to such approaches. In general terms although in many TVEI lessons pupils were 'active' and 'doing', they were often engaged in fact gathering, structured experimental activities, skills acquisition or discussion related to values clarification. Open ended problem solving where pupils controlled the activity or problems were found by them rather than given to them by the teacher, were rarely observed, with the exception of CDT/Technology project work. There were some difficulties observed in relation to values education. Many values issues were handled in discussion, often with teachers, but there was little evidence that strategies for values education had been clearly worked out. Thus teachers were not always able to facilitate pupils in clarifying values and sometimes inculcated values rather than explored them. Our observations would suggest that there is a space for more emphasis on open ended enquiry within TVEI where pupils are encouraged to research an issue or problem which requires them to make values and factual enquiries, so that they are able to make decisions which are reasoned value judgements. Many problems given to pupils in TVEI demand merely technical know-how to solve them and are not introducing pupils to the complexities of decision making in real life situations.

Reporting of Evaluation of Teaching and Learning Styles

Reporting of student perceptions, staff perceptions, work experience, in-service courses or 'exceptional' activities like mini-enterprise is straight forward by comparison with reporting classroom behaviour. Often the evaluator is dealing with perceptions — how satisfied people report themselves as being and any observations are of relatively public events. Recipients of reports are willing to examine an evaluation for the implications it has for their future work. The object of the evaluation is not deeply sensitive, it is relatively public and criteria for what counts as good or appropriate appear to be shared.

Classroom behaviour is sensitive — it is the very core of the teaching process and about the teacher as a person. It is not often an experience which is public or shared with other adults and when it is, as in team teaching, it becomes a very different experience. Finally, as has already been asserted, criteria for what counts as good teaching or TVEI teaching are not shared.

Evaluations which seek to serve decision-making at a number of levels need to communicate their findings so that meaning is communicated by the report, so that animosity is not aroused and so that the 'So what?' question can be constructively addressed.

Our experiences of reporting include a teacher breaking into tears, a co-ordinator defending teachers with the claim that any style of teaching was appropriate to TVEI, a teacher claiming the observer did not have the subject expertise to comment on the lesson and a headteacher withdrawing permission to use the material until some wording had been satisfactorily resolved.

The TRIST document (MSC, 1988) referred to earlier is an introductory attempt through 20 statements (and their opposites) to set out in specific terms what active learning looks like. However, it demands shared constructs to match the shared vocabulary. What actually counts as 'negotiation' and when is 'problem solving' not really 'problem solving'? What does a teacher do that counts as 'facilitating' and 'enabling' and what activities obstruct the teacher in doing this?

The vocabulary is taken very often on a rhetorical level — 'we all know what that means and that it is right'. Taxonomies, typologies and continua will not help evaluations to support development in teaching and learning styles in TVEI until they are expressed in highly specific terms which the teacher can relate unambiguously to his or her classroom experience. The notion of 'ownership of innovation' is appropriate here; teachers need to engage with the ideas and concepts so that they can understand the rhetoric and develop their classroom practices towards a style of teaching which they themselves have defined as appropriate. In this way teaching and learning styles can be developed appropriate to the circumstances in which teachers find themselves rather than urging them towards some 'ideal' yet ill-defined model.

The impact of an evaluation of teaching and learning styles is blunted at a number of points for a number of reasons. Firstly, such a focus for evaluation is intrusive and sensitive and relies on first hand data not self-report feedback through interview or questionnaire. It thus approaches the core of what it is to be a person in teaching. Secondly, and stemming from the point above, criticism can easily evoke antagonism and defensiveness. Thirdly, the lack of shared meaning makes clear communications, especially about specific features, difficult. Fourthly, if the preceding stages have not been adequately managed it is difficult to decide on action to promote development for the recipients of the evaluation.

The Leeds National Evaluation Unit has given impetus to studies of classroom behaviour. Local evaluators need to approach studies of classrooms with much more precise focuses which prompt discussion about and give rise to proposals about *specific* features and indicate *precise focuses* for in-service trainings, and still not lose sight of the holistic nature of teaching.

References

BARNES, D., JOHNSON, G., JORDAN, S., LAYTON, D., MEDWAY, P. & YEOMANS, D. 1987, *The TVEI Curriculum 14–16*. London: Training Agency.

BARTLETT, L. & COX, B. 1982, *Learning to Teach Geography*. Australia: John Wiley.

MSC 1988, *Paper of National Interest 6. TRIST New Approaches to Teaching and Learning*. London: Training Agency.

7 Outcomes of change in teaching and learning style

RICHARD D. HAZELWOOD
School of Education,
University of Newcastle

Introduction

In the introduction to his book about TVEI, Denis Gleeson (Gleeson, 1987) put teaching and learning style firmly in its place as a major element of TVEI:

> In essence the project may be viewed as an attempt at major innovation to stimulate curriculum development and to introduce new approaches to teaching and learning.

The notion of this new emphasis is to be encountered throughout the literature and has been on the lips of most of those closely associated with the project. In the TVEI Review of 1985 Brian Nicholson suggested that projects were

> introducing changes in teaching styles. Increasingly these are geared towards providing students with the opportunity to develop initiative, motivation, problem solving skills . . . . Central to this approach is the transfer to students themselves of more responsibility for managing their own learning (Nicholson, 1985).

Others have referred to teacher-assisted learning and a project-based approach (e.g. Wind, 1986) and active learning with an emphasis on experience (Harland, 1987). Many of the fears initially expressed by teachers of the interventionist, political nature of the initiative (see e.g. Saunders, 1986; Fiddy, 1988) subsided as the emphasis moved from the vocational and training aspect to what was seen as the more sound educational area of teaching and learning style, a move well summarised by Gleeson & Smith:

> . . . the bottom up nature of TVEI has ensured that rather than being 'New Vocationalism', TVEI is becoming more and more 'New Educationalism' (Gleeson & Smith, 1987).

In attending regional TVEI co-ordinators' meetings and MSC Reviews it became apparent that, apart from some management issues (inevitably important in the early days) teaching and learning was the major emphasis and many evaluators went along with this emphasis. In a poll of eight TVEI local evaluators in October 1985 teaching and learning style emerged as the area which they felt was most important to examine (Tree & Hazelwood, 1985). This emphasis was not really surprising — when some of the elements of TVEI were less easy to comprehend this aspect did reflect a trend already present in education and the majority (but by no means all) of teachers saw the proposed changes as a progressive step in the right direction. Later, of course, GCSE adopted a similar emphasis continuing the trend.

What Evidence is There of a Real Change?

Certainly there is a wealth of case study and interview evidence suggesting that TVEI has brought about changes in the classroom. Local evaluators encountered considerable enthusiasm for the new approach to learning and saw many examples of good practice. By 1987 we felt justified in statements such as: 'there was a clear indication of a real change in some classrooms' (McCabe & Hazelwood, 1987). But there lies the crunch — 'in some classrooms'. There is no doubt that in a climate of innovation fuelled by unprecedented levels of funding there were some highly innovative and successful developments — usually in the hands of teachers who often stated that they were moving in a direction they had always wanted to go. But how representative were these pockets of 'good practice' (TVEI was being judged at that stage largely on the basis of implementation, i.e. if it was happening it was successful). How different were the lessons for the majority of TVEI pupils? Some unease about the subjective nature of much evidence was recently voiced in the Training Commission publication *TVEI Insight* (quoting as an example: 'there appears to be a wide consensus across reports that students have generally enjoyed their work experience') in which Jack Cross suggested that such statements serve little in analytic terms, and can hardly be considered evaluative in any meaningful sense (Cross, 1988). The degree of change may not have been as great as many have imagined. Douglas Barnes (Barnes, 1987) noted that in six schools studied in depth using classroom observations 'only two undeniable examples of the negotiated pedagogy' were found. Haywood & Tymms (1988) observing more than 50 lessons found none *negotiated* and more than half *controlled*. However, there is some evidence that TVEI students were experiencing a different style in the classroom. In a study of over 2,000 TVEI students Hazelwood, Fitz-Gibbon & McCabe (1988) found that they had perceived a more student-centred approach with emphasis on group work, discussion and activities outside school and correspondingly less traditional and didactic approaches. The size of the effect was not great but had statistical significance for most items in the questionnaire used. Table 7.1 comes from that paper.

As researchers we are well aware of the difficulty of capturing in hard data what seems apparent to all (see Brickell, 1976) and bearing in mind that since the questionnaire referred to lessons in general not TVEI lessons it seems probable that real and larger differences were present and that the good practice found in the case studies was having an effect on student perception.

What are the Outcomes?

There seems to be case study evidence that some students have enjoyed their school work more. Certainly we have encountered considerable enthusiasm when interviewing students in the course of our activities but have no way of knowing how representative these perceptions are or how those students would have responded without TVEI. Harris (1988) in a survey of students and parents did confirm a high level of commitment in TVEI pupils but in a large scale survey of over 3,800 pupils TVEI pupils reported enjoying their lessons slightly less than non-TVEI pupils (Hazelwood & Fitz-Gibbon, 1987). After almost two years of TVEI a survey of most of those same pupils revealed little change in this finding (Fitz-Gibbon, Hazelwood, McCabe & Tymms, 1988). However, could it have been that there were real differences not revealed by making TVEI/non-TVEI comparisons? Re-analysis comparing groups of students reporting the most and the least experiential experiences suggested that experiential learning was associated with increased enjoyment (Hazelwood, 1988a) — perhaps the pupils who actually experienced a TVEI approach (whether or not they were in the official cohort) showed more enjoyment. It is worth recording that many teachers have reported finding teaching using a more student-centred approach more rewarding.

There is little evidence that these approaches lead to increased learning. Fitz-Gibbons *et al.* (1988) showed a depression of conventional examination results by TVEI and Hazelwood (1988a) showed no statistically significant effect of experiential learning on exam results. Of course one could argue that new examination methods which reflect the teaching methodology will better assess its outcomes — this may well become the case but it would be surprising if a system which involved more teacher assessment didn't lead to 'better' results.

TABLE 7.1 *Group mean responses to teaching and learning style items*[a]

	TVEI	*Non-TVEI*	*Non-Non-TVEI*
n	*436*	*1204*	*371*
1. We work with others in a group.	3.37	3.22*	3.22* +
2. We work with just one other person.	3.00	3.01	2.72*
3. We work on our own.	3.36	3.49*	3.52* +
4. We often break up into small groups.	2.94	2.79*	2.53* +
5. The teacher tells us what we should know and we write it down.	3.36	3.41	3.55* +
6. The teacher likes us to find answers to problems ourselves.	3.81	3.83	3.80
7. We have opportunities to use equipment.	3.66	3.43*	3.29* +
8. We spend our time discussing our work.	3.13	3.15	3.23
9. We listen to the teacher or read from a course book.	3.41	3.54*	3.79* +
10. We can decide for ourselves what to work on.	2.22	2.12	2.09* +
11. We work at our own pace on projects.	3.51	3.43	3.49
12. The teacher dictates a lot of notes for us to write down.	3.03	3.08	3.22* +
13. How much have you discussed your progress as school with your teachers?	2.37	2.25	2.47
14. Has your school work involved activities outside school?	3.04	2.82*	2.77* +
15. In school have you learned skills which will be useful in getting a job?	3.83	3.63*	3.64* +

Notes:
[a] Responses were on a five point Likert scale.
+ indicates support for the hypothesis that TVEI students experienced a more student-centred less didactic learning situation.
* indicates significantly different from the TVEI group.

Perhaps what is required is a more experimental approach. 'Heads Didactic/Tails Experiential' was an interesting and well received example of TVEI INSET which arose from discussions with local advisers about the merits of different teaching and learning styles and is a good example of LEA/University co-operation. Teachers attended a three day course which gave an introduction to the experimental approach, where they discussed and considered the operationalisation of different styles of teaching. Pairs of teachers were randomly assigned to teach a series of lessons experientially or didactically (Hazelwood & Fitz-Gibbon, 1988). Attitude and cognitive pre- and post-tests were given to the pupils. A follow-up day was used to discuss the experience, its findings and their validity. In three out of five experiments the greater learning was in the didactic group, and in three out of five the experiential group expressed more interest in the work. There seems little doubt that evaluative skills are going to be increasingly required of teachers and the major success of this project was the experience for those who developed and conducted the experiments but we should not ignore the results though on such a small scale they must be treated with caution (see Table 7.2 for a summary of the results).

Mixed Methods are Best

In order to produce some change it may well have been necessary to overstate the case for 'new' styles of teaching and learning. But let us be careful not to accept the overstatements without question. Any movement which increases the repertoire of teachers is of benefit but should retain the best of what went before. Perhaps we should adopt an interpretation of student-centred learning proposed by Rob Fiddy (1988) and define it as 'the most effective form within the situation, whether it be active, passive, experiential or didactic'. We should see the movement as a slow shift towards a more experiential approach but not towards replacing one approach with another, because there is little hard evidence that one is superior to the other. Douglas Barnes (1987) seems to infer this notion of a slow shift:

> It is my view that teachers whose normal teaching methods could be called Controlled should ask themselves whether they should be reaching toward a Framed pedagogy, and those who are already comfortable in using a Framed method might consider whether there are not occasions when they can aid their students in taking more

responsibility, and even attempt joint planning of part of a course with them.

It is enlightening to consider how teachers prefer to be taught themselves. In recent evaluations of INSET activity (Hazelwood, 1988a) it was apparent that not all teachers prefer active, experiential learning. Approximately one third of the teachers in the studies stated that they would rather have been told — i.e. have been given information, in effect instructed. Why should we believe students are any different? Not all students are comfortable in the participative, active situation and we should not assume that it is the role of teachers to enforce that mode of learning on all regardless. Surely what is required is a curriculum, timetable and support which allow teachers to experiment but does not regard success only in terms of one mode of learning. Indeed in many ways the funding of the TVEI pilot, and the time created by it, provided just this freedom, but now is not the time to say we have learned the lessons and that we must get on and enforce, or encourage, one learning mode, for the lessons have been different depending upon the individual teacher and the students.

TABLE 7.2 *Heads didactic/tails experiential — Summary results*

Pair	*Method*[a]		*Attitude Change*[b]		*Learning*[c]	
	E	*D*	*E*	*D*	*E*	*D*
1	55	46	2.7	–0.4	–15*	14
2	63*	35	–3.7*	9.5	7.4*	–2.3
3	64*	32	3.3	–12	9.0*	20
4	65*	49	3.1	1.4	10	13
5	73*	32	–0.2	–0.5	11	11
ALL	66*	36	0	0	6	9

Notes:
[a] Indicates Extent of Treatment Differences based on pupil ratings on a number of items.
[b] Post minus Pre Attitude index.
[c] Post minus Pre Cognitive scores.
* indicates significant at 0.05 level.
E = Experiential, D = Didactic

It would seem that a teacher who mixes his/her methods as appropriate to the topic is doing as much as we can reasonably ask. In that way variety is achieved and the various learning preferences of different students are catered for.

References

BARNES, D. 1987, A first impression of TVEI in six schools. In D. GLEESON, (ed.), *TVEI and Secondary Education: A Critical Appraisal* (pp. 141–52). Milton Keynes: Open University Press.

BRICKELL, H. M. 1976, Instruments as good as our eyes. *Journal of Career Education* 2(3), 56–66.

CROSS, J. 1988, 'Reviews'. *TVEI Insight*. p. 29.

FIDDY, R. 1988, TVEI in Essex and Suffolk: Final Report. Centre for Applied Research in Education. UEA Norwich (mimeo).

FITZ-GIBBON, C., HAZELWOOD, R., MCCABE, C. & TYMMS, P. 1988, Performance Indicators and the TVEI Pilot. *Evaluation and Research in Education* 2(2), 49–60.

GLEESON, D. (ed.) 1987, *TVEI and Secondary Education: A Critical Appraisal*. Milton Keynes: Open University Press.

GLEESON, D. & SMITH, G. 1987, 16–18: The neglected territory of TVEI. In D. GLEESON (ed.) *TVEI and Secondary Education: A Critical Appraisal* (pp. 141–52). Milton Keynes: Open University Press.

HARLAND, J. 1987, The TVEI experience: Issues of control, response, and the professional role of teachers. In D. GLEESON (ed.) *TVEI and Secondary Education: A Critical Appraisal* (pp. 38–54). Milton Keynes: Open University Press.

HARRIS, D. 1987, Consulting the customers: A strategy for the development of TVEI. *Evaluation and Research in Education* 1(3), 131–46.

HAYWOOD, R. & TYMMS, P. 1988, A report based on classroom observation. Unpublished evaluation report, CEM, School of Education, University of Newcastle (mimeo).

HAZELWOOD, R. 1988a, Performance indicators for student-centred learning (Presented at BERA conference). School of Education, University of Newcastle (mimeo).

— INSET evaluation. Unpublished Report, CEM, School of Education, University of Newcastle (mimeo).

HAZELWOOD, R. & FITZ-GIBBON, C. 1987, Analysis of large scale data collection. Unpublished Report, CEM, School of Education, University of Newcastle (mimeo).

— 1988, Heads didactic, tails experiential. Unpublished Report, CEM, School of Education, University of Newcastle (mimeo).

HAZELWOOD, R., FITZ-GIBBON, C. & MCCABE, C. 1988, Student perception of teaching and learning styles. *Evaluation and Research in Education* 2 (2), 61–8.

MCCABE, C. & HAZELWOOD, R. 1987, Long term perception of TVEI. Unpublished Report, CEM, School of Education, University of Newcastle (mimeo).

NICHOLSON, B. 1985, *TVEI Review*. London: MSC.

SAUNDERS, M. 1986, Managing the enclave. In C. MCCABE (ed.), *TVEI: The Organisation of the Early Years*. Clevedon, Avon: Multilingual Matters.

TREE, A. & HAZELWOOD, R. 1985, A common focus for TVEI evaluation. Discussion Document, CEM, School of Education, University of Newcastle (mimeo).

WIND, B. 1986, A 14–16 Modular Core. *TVEI Developments*. London: MSC.

Note: A number of documents referred to are local evaluation reports (produced at the Curriculum Evaluation and Management Centre, School of Education, University of Newcastle upon Tyne) which could only be made available after negotiation with the parties concerned.

8 TVEI pilots in profile

GILL HELSBY
Institute for Research and Development in Post-Compulsory Education, University of Lancaster

From the outset, 'profiling' has been a feature of TVEI pilot schemes. Although the actual practice has varied widely from area to area and even from school to school, it has generally had two recognisable characteristics. On the one hand there has been a concern to introduce an on-going and formative process of student review and guidance. On the other attention has focused upon the production of a summative document, or record of achievement, for school leavers.

Certainly the original criteria for TVEI effectively specify that both formative and summative aspects of profiling should be included. Despite some ambiguity in the TVEI extension criteria over the summative document, their clear implication is that profiling should be extended from a pilot group to all students. This would be in line with the DES Policy Statement on Records of Achievement (July 1984) which itself goes well beyond the stipulation for a written record for all school leavers, and clearly implies student involvement in reviewing and recording throughout their secondary school careers.

It might well be assumed from the criteria for TVEI extension that the case for formative profiling had been proved by experiences in the TVEI pilot scheme. Certainly it would seem to have generated a good deal of enthusiastic debate amongst teachers and educationalists. Conversations with teachers already involved in profiling, however, provoke a fairly mixed response. Whilst some are enthusiastic — or even evangelical — about the perceived benefits, many express serious reservations about the amount of time involved. Some have described profiling as an 'unrealistic pipe dream' within existing structures, whilst others are openly cynical about its objectives. Generally, however, the major difficulties in this area are seen in terms of *teacher* problems rather than *student* problems.

In the event, recent surveys of students with regard to both their pre-16 and post-16 educational experiences suggest that profiling receives a fairly mixed welcome from its recipients and assumed beneficiaries. The first survey was conducted amongst some 3,000 students across 12 TVEI Authorities. The respondents were aged between 16 and 17: some had remained in full-time education, but many had left school and were now employed, unemployed or on a Youth Training Scheme. All were asked to reflect back upon their experiences in the fifth year. Three quarters of those who had been TVEI students at 14–16 said that they had regularly filled in a profile, compared to one in five of the non-TVEI respondents.

In the questionnaire, a number of statements were made about profiling, and those who had been involved were asked to respond to these statements on a five point scale ranging from 'strongly agree' to 'strongly disagree'.

From this data, student responses to profiling appear to be very ambivalent. As can be seen from Figure 8.1, only about a quarter of respondents thought that profiling had helped to improve their schoolwork, more disagreed than agreed that it had aided self-understanding and two-thirds doubted whether their profile would help them get a job if they showed it to an employer. On the other hand, nearly a half of respondents said that they could see the point of profiling and did not think that it was too much effort for what they got out of it.

When considering whether or not teachers should feel discouraged by these results, three factors must be borne in mind. The first is that the proportions given represent the mean across 12 different TVEI schemes: in some LEAs respondents were considerably more positive about profiling, whilst in others they were obviously more negative. From the consumers' point of view, feelings about profiling (and presumably therefore practices) vary from scheme to scheme. In some areas it can, apparently, be successful.

Secondly, it must be borne in mind that two thirds of our respondents were in the first cohort of TVEI students. In many cases, therefore, profiling was in its first two years of operation, when staff awareness, experience and counselling skills were still developing. It could well be that the systems are working differently now.

The third factor is concerned with the limitations of a written questionnaire. The answers cannot tell us how students interpreted 'profiling'. There is no way, for instance, of knowing whether those who answered our questions were thinking of it as simply a paper-filling exercise or whether they were taking into account any associated counselling sessions.

	Agree %	*Disagree %*
Profiling helped me to improve my schoolwork	27.4	48.2
Profiling helped me to understand myself better	35.8	39.5
Profiling helped me to get on better with the teachers	42.6	34.6
I think my profile would help me get a job if I showed it to an employer	34.6	38.1
Profiling helped me decide what job I wanted to do	7.9	75.1
Profiling was too much effort for what I got out of it	29.1	45.3
I couldn't see the point of profiling	34.0	47.9
I never really knew what to put in my profile	35.9	45.9
Profiling made me feel uncomfortable	19.5	54.1
Profiling seemed to make teachers feel uncomfortable	4.8	59.5
The teachers didn't give me a chance to say what I wanted	13.3	72.4
Teachers seemed really keen on profiling	48.1	22.2
We were meant to do profiling but we didn't do it much	32.0	52.6
There wasn't enough time to do it properly	37.9	46.3

FIGURE 8.1 *Views on profiling in the fifth form*

Given, however, the amount of time and money that is often devoted to profiling, these mixed responses do raise a number of serious questions about some of the assumed purposes of the exercise. These are questions which really ought to be answered before rushing into the extension of profiling to all students.

From the early days of profiling, there has always been a tension between 'process' and 'product', between on-going, formative review and the production of a summative end document which could be presented to employers or to gatekeepers in further or higher education. Our questionnaire tried to take into account both aspects, with key questions on the effects of the process and the perceived usefulness of the product.

It is interesting that only about 35% of our respondents felt that their profile could help them get a job if they showed it to an employer, whilst nearly 38% positively disagreed with this suggestion. At the present time their scepticism may well be justified, since there is as yet very little evidence about the use of profiles by employers. Indeed the MSC/Training Agency and DES have funded a research study in this area.

Given this uncertainty, it is perhaps unfortunate that a lot of development time is sometimes given over to consideration of the end document, that a number of teachers still see it as one of the main purposes of profiling and that many claim that it has an undue influence upon the formative process.

If students were not convinced about the usefulness of the final document, were they more confident about the benefits of the process? One of the aims of TVEI is the personal development of students, and it is often claimed that profiling has an important part to play in this development. Certainly the DES Policy Statement of 1984 stated that this was one of the four purposes of records of achievement, which should 'contribute to pupils' personal development and progress by improving their motivation, providing encouragement and increasing their awareness of strengths, weaknesses and opportunities'.

Our questionnaire asked respondents whether they thought that profiling had helped them to understand themselves better. Here opinions varied, and whilst in one of the twelve LEAs 66% of respondents thought that it had, overall nearly two-thirds expressed some doubt.

It may be, of course, that students find difficulty not only in identifying gains in self-understanding, but also in seeing a link between that and profiling. On the other hand, it may be that some teachers see profiling as primarily a means of recording information for their own benefit and/or reporting to parents and other outside users, and therefore approach it as a largely one-sided activity.

If personal development through increased self-understanding is to be an aim of profiling, it seems clear that this aim must be made explicit and must be shared by the teachers involved. Equally it is difficult to imagine this aim being achieved without the fairly close involvement of students. If this is to happen, there are obvious time and resource implications (which may not always be met).

One of the justifications for making time available for profiling is the assumed enhancement of student learning. However, when asked whether profiling had helped to improve their schoolwork, only about a quarter of our respondents agreed, whilst nearly a half disagreed.

Once again, the pattern of responses varied from area to area. In two LEAs, indeed, almost half of the students (i.e. double the average) did see a connection between profiling and improved schoolwork. The picture overall, however, is not particularly encouraging.

There are strong arguments as to why profiling should be rooted in student learning rather than in personal development. In their interim report (November 1987) the Records of Achievement National Steering committee claim that the integration of records into the main curriculum is crucial if the necessary changes in school structures and staff attitudes are to be achieved. As they point out: 'If records are confined to the pastoral side only, they will be seen as peripheral.'

Conversations with teachers involved in profiling for TVEI suggest, however, that many subject teachers may well see profiling as very much the responsibility of the (pastoral?) profiling tutor. Consequently they may regard their role as simply providing information to support any external tutorial sessions, rather than seeing profiling as an integral part of the teaching and learning process. In this situation, involvement in profiling becomes an additional chore, particularly in cases where teachers are also expected to produce traditional reports to parents.

It is fair to add that the fact that large numbers of students did not see a connection between profiling and improved work need not mean that that connection does not exist. What it does suggest, however, is that schools need to find out more about why students feel like this before extending profiling further.

Respondents to our questionnaire were also asked about the way profiling was conducted and how they felt about it. The majority of those involved thought that they had had a say in deciding what went into their profile. Nearly 30% claimed that they had themselves been responsible for the decisions, whilst over half thought that it had been a joint enterprise with teachers. Only 12% felt that their teachers had not given them the chance to say what they wanted to say in profiling sessions.

One in five respondents said that profiling made them feel uncomfortable, and this was more likely to apply to boys than to girls. Very few, however, thought that their teachers seemed awkward about it: indeed nearly a half thought that their teachers were really keen on the idea!

Almost one in three agreed that they did not do a lot of profiling even though they were meant to, whilst 38% thought that there wasn't enough time to do it properly. Surprisingly, well over a third of respondents (mostly girls) claimed that they never knew what to put in their profile.

It is tempting to assume that many of this group were thinking of log books or diaries when they answered that question, since our research suggests that these are unpopular with students. It has been suggested that many of the problems in this area centred on the question of confidentiality and trust between students and teachers. Comments from our respondents simply underlined the fact that log books were seen as boring and pointless:

> '. . . in my opinion the log book didn't do anything to help me and I found it hard to write in it.'
> 'TVEI log books are boring and a waste of time.'
> 'As far as I am concerned, all I got from TVEI was a stupid little yellow log book which was used to give you something to talk about in the rare interviews with the course tutor.'

To turn now to the positive side of student responses to our questions, an encouraging 48% of respondents overall said that they could see the point of profiling, and this figure rose to over 70% in one particular LEA. At the same time, over 45% overall disagreed that profiling had been too much effort for what they got out of it. Moreover on average more than four out of ten respondents agreed that profiling had helped them get on better with teachers, a figure which in some areas rose to six or even seven out of ten. In all of these cases, girls were somewhat more positive than boys (see Figure 8.2).

From the consumers' point of view, it is not clear from the survey what the more positive students see as the main purpose of profiling, nor what they think that they gain from it. Certainly this information was not volunteered in the 'open comments' section at the end of the questionnaire. We are left to suppose that it is a combination of better relationships with teachers, greater self-understanding, a belief in the usefulness of a profile when applying for a job and/or confidence that it can help to improve schoolwork.

	Agree %		*Disagree %*	
	M	*F*	*M*	*F*
Profiling helped me to improve my schoolwork	26.0	29.0	50.6	45.8
Profiling helped me to understand myself better	33.3	38.7	42.3	36.5
Profiling helped me to get on better with the teachers	41.6	44.1	32.1	36.7
I think my profile would help me get a job if I showed it to an employer	32.5	36.7	41.1	34.7
Profiling helped me decide what job I wanted to do	7.2	8.4	74.3	76.0
Profiling was too much effort for what I got out of it	32.4	25.2	41.8	48.7
I couldn't see the point of profiling	36.5	31.4	44.8	51.1
I never really knew what to put in my profile	6.8	35.4	43.7	48.5
Profiling made me feel uncomfortable	22.7	15.7	50.6	57.9
Profiling seemed to make teachers feel uncomfortable	7.5	2.2	54.6	64.4
The teachers didn't give me a chance to say what I wanted	15.6	10.8	68.4	76.1
Teachers seemed really keen on profiling	47.2	48.4	23.5	21.4
We were meant to do profiling but we didn't do it much	34.1	30.3	49.2	55.4
There wasn't enough time to do it properly	37.7	37.5	47.3	44.8

FIGURE 8.2 *Views on profiling in the fifth form: gender differences*

A later survey was conducted amongst some 1,000 TVEI students in their second year of post-16 education. Although a smaller proportion of this age group had been regularly involved in profiling, their attitudes towards the experience were somewhat more positive. Thus, over half of them claimed that profiling had helped them to understand their strengths and weaknesses better and that they could see the point of the exercise. Nearly one in three felt that it had had a positive effect upon their academic performance, whilst nearly a half agreed that they would show their final profile to an employer or to a college or university admissions tutor (see Figure 8.3).

	Agree %	*Disagree %*
Profiling helped me to understand my strengths and weaknesses better	54.0	28.8
Profiling helped me to improve in my studies	30.4	45.0
I got on better with teachers because of profiling	29.3	45.0
I would show my final profile to a potential employer or to a college or university tutor	44.5	32.0
I couldn't really see the point of profiling	25.3	55.2
I found it useful writing about my experiences	45.1	33.6
Filling in the profile took up too much time	32.3	49.8
Doing the profiling is more important than the final document	22.6	37.2
I enjoyed the interviews/reviews/counselling sessions	38.3	30.4
We spent a lot of time on profiling	22.6	62.9
The time spent on profiling could have been better spent in studying	33.6	42.9
There is never enough time to do the profiling properly	33.3	42.4
Teachers seem really keen on profiling	40.8	27.5

FIGURE 8.3 *Views of profiling in post-16 students*

Interestingly, however, they were less convinced than the younger students that profiling had helped to improve relationships with teachers, and there seemed to be a slightly greater emphasis upon the usefulness of writing about experiences than upon the benefits and enjoyment of one-to-one interviews.

Differences in response according to gender were more marked in this age group than amongst the younger students. As can be seen from Figure 8.4, girls were in most respects noticeably more positive than boys about the benefits of profiling, and they claim to have spent more time on it. They are, however, slightly less likely than boys to agree that they got on better with teachers because of profiling.

These responses cannot 'prove' anything about profiling, partly because of the limitations of a written questionnaire and partly because they are the views of only one of the parties involved in the process. None the less, students are the ones who are supposed to gain from profiling, and we should not ignore their views.

The responses do, I believe, reflect upon some of the difficulties inherent in developing a profiling system. Such difficulties have emerged not only through the experiences of TVEI pilot, but also within the DES pilot schemes for Records of Achievement. In both cases they stem, almost certainly, from the fact that successful profiling is not an isolated, 'bolt-on' activity that can be easily accommodated within existing structures. If it is to be meaningful, two factors have to be taken into account:

1. In as far as it involves the assessment of a wide range of skills, it is inextricably linked with the whole curriculum.
2. In as far as it broadens the range of what is assessed and focuses upon student achievement in those broad areas, it directly challenges conventional teaching methodology.

Accordingly its introduction is unlikely to be painless, whilst its full development is likely to be slow.

It must be emphasised that there is nothing inherently difficult in the idea of profiling itself. It is quite logical for a school or college to seek to assess and record a wide range of student skills and abilities provided that these reflect the main teaching and learning objectives, and that appropriate strategies are adopted to achieve those ends. Didactic approaches, for example, may be unhelpful when students need to practice, develop and demonstrate skills, whilst directive teaching may foster dependency rather than initiative. It could be argued that the major difficulties that occur in profiling arise less from any innate flaws in the concept, and more

	Agree %		*Disagree %*	
	M	*F*	*M*	*F*
Profiling helped me to understand my strengths and weaknesses better	50.8	56.5	32.5	26.1
Profiling helped me to improve in my studies	23.6	35.3	48.3	42.5
I got on better with teachers because of profiling	31.5	27.6	42.3	46.9
I would show my final profile to a potential employer or to a college or university tutor	39.8	47.8	39.8	26.2
I couldn't really see the point of profiling	30.1	21.8	47.8	60.7
I found it useful writing about my experiences	34.8	52.5	39.3	29.5
Filling in the profile took up too much time	32.1	32.6	50.2	49.4
Doing the profiling is more important than the final document	19.7	24.7	39.9	35.3
I enjoyed the interviews/reviews/ counselling sessions	34.0	41.3	33.5	28.3
We spent a lot of time on profiling	15.9	27.5	73.7	55.0
The time spent of profiling could have been better spent in studying	37.4	30.7	38.9	45.7
There is never enough time to do the profiling properly	32.1	34.1	42.4	42.5
Teachers seem really keen on profiling	37.9	42.9	31.8	24.4

FIGURE 8.4 *Views on profiling in post-16 students: gender differences*

as a result of a mismatch between the profiling objectives, the curriculum-as-it-is-taught and the teaching methodology.

On a more specific and practical level, however, we did interview students in one LEA where responses to profiling had appeared fairly negative. Here we discovered a much more basic and fundamental reason why they may have responded in the way that they did. In two schools, profiling took the form of interviews with a profiling tutor. These interviews were relatively isolated from normal lessons and, because they were conducted by a single profiling tutor, fairy infrequent: over the two years from 14–16 students had had, on average, two to three 10 minute interviews. In this context, it is surely hardly surprising that students would claim that it had had little influence on their schoolwork, on self-understanding or on relationships with teachers. Although few objected to the interviews, and many enjoyed them, their infrequency and their detachment from normal lessons meant that, in the words of students, they were 'no big thing'.

On the positive side, responses to our questionnaire did indicate that profiling could be very successful in some cases. At its best, nearly 50% of respondents in one LEA thought that profiling in the fifth form had helped them to improve their schoolwork, 66% claimed that it had aided self-understanding whilst 70% felt that it had helped to improve relationships with teachers and said that they could see the point of the exercise. With regard to the final document, well over a half were confident that it might help them to get a job if they showed it to an employer.

The next stage will be to undertake further research in LEAs where the responses were more positive, with a view to trying to identify elements of good practice which might be replicable elsewhere. Some factors are already apparent: in the more 'successful' authorities, profiling was given a high status from the beginning. Overt support came from both the LEA and from senior management teams in schools. Generally a profiling co-ordinator of senior status was appointed in each institution, and a good deal of time was devoted to the activity.

Perhaps the inevitable conclusion at the moment is a simple one: the gains from profiling are commensurate with the degree of investment. If that investment is small, then the results are likely to be disappointing. If it is large, then there is much to be gained.

Unfortunately, however, we are left with a chicken and egg situation: schools and colleges have to be convinced that the gains are sufficient to justify a large investment. How can they be convinced, unless and until they have experienced some of those gains?

References

DES/Welsh Office 1984 (July), Records of achievement: A statement of policy.

— 1987 (November), Records of achievement: An interim report from the National Steering Committee.

9 Profiling: Time and ownership

JOHN BEATTIE
School of Education,
University of Newcastle

The first response of any teacher to a question about profiling is to reply that there isn't enough time. The second response is that there isn't enough physical space. This latter problem is to some extent a sub-category of the question of time; where this is so there have been attempts to provide suitable accommodation, often funded directly by TVEI, where the delicate process of negotiation can take place. Nevertheless, in any analysis of profiling the question of time must be seen as the critical one. (By profiling here the formative aspect only is being considered and not the production of the final record of achievement.) Nowhere was it put better than in a recent annual review where one headteacher commented, 'God created the world in seven days but even he did not allow sufficient time for profiling'. The purpose of this chapter is to explore recent developments in profiling in one pilot scheme, in particular the way in which the vexed question of time has been dealt with. If, however, time is the teacher's concern, the evaluator is increasingly focusing on ownership as the crucial factor in our understanding of the development of profiling.

One of the characteristics of the pilot scheme is that, in common with several others, it appointed a central team of support teachers in important curriculum areas, through which the development of TVEI would take place. This team which became known as the curriculum co-ordinators worked in IT, Technology, Business Studies and P.S.E. Under the general heading of P.S.E. was included the brief for the development of profiling in the consortium schools. This inclusion represents a realistic appreciation of the likely development of profiling in the consortium schools. This inclusion represents a realistic appreciation of the likely development of profiling rather than a statement of an ideology of profiling. For unimportant reasons the appointment of the P.S.E. curriculum co-ordinator did not take place until the January of the first year of the pilot. Therefore the early development of profiling was in the hands of the TVEI co-ordinator. It must be recalled that TVEI co-ordinators were not in the first place appointed for their skills in the area of pastoral care or their expert knowledge of profiling. They were appointed in the most part for some TVEI relevant expertise and for a sympathy to the aims of TVEI, which in this context included P.S.E. and profiling. To say that there had been no profiling in the consortium schools would be to underestimate the work done by individuals and to underplay the level of awareness of profiling at the level of senior management in all the schools which became involved in the scheme. It was against this background of well directed enthusiasm that the P.S.E. co-ordinator was asked to develop a formative profile and a summative profile for those who would go into employment or to the 6th form/FE college at 16+. Working from what was known by the teachers in their pilot, the P.S.E. curriculum co-ordinator began to adapt the well known CGLI 365 profile as a basis for development. Many pilot schemes have adopted the diary, in a fairly prestigious form, as an important part of the formative profiling process. It would seem that the possession of a slim folder, closely resembling a FILOFAX, would confer on the TVEI student, not only a special status but also a special desire to do well.

The integration of the diary and the cross-curricular 365 profile would seem a sensible place to start. It is possible to take 12 cross-curricular skills, arranged as in the 365, group them in threes and construct a rotation system that would enable students to attempt to have all of them accredited monthly. If this was linked to a diary that both looked to school work and extra curricular expertise and activities, and stressed at each stage reflection about the past and hopes for the future, then there would be a real chance that the process of profiling could happen. The system of formative profiling would be completed by the addition of a subject specific profile which would itemise recently completed learning targets in a module or section, contain a statement from both teacher and pupil about progress in these areas and an agreed and negotiated target for the pupil. Besides the paper accumulated as a record of current progress a crucial aspect of this profiling system would be reliance for its initiation on the student. There are two aspects to this. It is clear that for this to work the ownership must be with the pupil and importantly, because this is a pilot and not all teachers would be equally committed, or well informed, initiation at teacher level would be thought unlikely. In the event, this latter assumption proved to be correct for the cross-curricular skills component of the profile.

To sum up then, the profile package which constituted the process consisted of:

> 12 cross-curricular skills linked to a diary with 4 or 5 subject specific profiles with attainment targets all this mediated through forms of tutorial support.

This package was developed by the P.S.E. curriculum co-ordinator, working through a group of interested teachers and was adopted across the consortium in the second year of the pilot.

To help this discussion certain aspects of this profiling process may be considered separately although in reality they are interwoven, and inter-dependent. Across the pilot scheme the dynamics of this inter-relationship varied. The crucial aspects would seem to be (a) the pastoral structure within the school which could support a profiling process, (b) the process of staff development, (c) the complexity of the scheme and the ownership of the authorship of the profiling process.

It is worthwhile considering these aspects separately.

The Pastoral Structure

In some schools the TVEI cohort was considered an exclusive group for all or most of its activities. They were taught as discrete groups in the subjects designated as TVEI and were treated in a special way for the core, which often included profiling. In the first years of the project existing structures were used to enable profiling to take place. Where the TVEI co-ordinator was also involved in P.S.E. or what was previously called 'Careers', time could be found to accommodate the cross-curricular profiling process. It must be stressed, however, that this time was found at lunch times and after school, and furthermore occurred during the 'teachers' dispute'. Valuable lessons were learned during this time, a few of which helped to solve the problem of time. What became clear for the 11–16 schools was that the year tutor structure was proving, over time, inadequate to support a real profiling process. (By a real profiling process is meant one which involves negotiation between the participants about agreed targets over a period of time and the constant evaluation and review of achievement and target setting.) In some of the schools year-groups are passed on from one tutor to the next. Where the cross-curricular profiling is completed by the form tutor in tutorial or P.S.E. time it is becoming apparent that the subtleties of the profiling process cannot be achieved with this structure. Commonly year tutors will comment that it takes at least two years to get to know a pupil well enough to be able to conduct a valid profiling interview. The learning is a two way process and as one teacher forcefully asserted at the beginning of the pilot: 'Fourth years are impossible to negotiate with and the worst people to negotiate with them are fourth year tutors'.

The structure which has emerged most commonly within the scheme in the 11–16 schools is a tutorial system which maximises continuity for the year tutors in the last three years of schooling. The first two years of school life for pupils are served by one tutor and the final three by another. Where profiling is performed by the year tutor this structure ensures the quality of the profiling process. In some schools the problem of lack of time for cross-curricular profiling has been partially solved by the TVEI co-ordinator assisting the year tutor by taking the tutorial part of P.S.E. sessions, thus liberating the tutor for the profiling work. In many schools this is seen as a temporary measure and does have the effect of demoting P.S.E. and emphasising the bolt-on nature of some profiling schemes. In some schools, almost all of what could be considered under a general heading of profiling is carried out by the TVEI co-ordinator. This is clearly the least satisfactory of all the arrangements.

As pilot schools are looking towards extension and wishing to bring to all pupils a profiling experience, supportive structures need to be further developed which will ensure that the process is integrated into the educational experience of the student.

Staff Development

At the start of the scheme very few teachers in the pilot had any experience of profiling. Those that had were limited to working with groups of children taking CGLI 365 scheme. The experience was thus inevitably restricted to the less able and there was considerable cynicism about the possibility of applying profiling across the ability range and in particular to the most able. Following the development of the consortium-wide profiling scheme in the first year, the start of the year saw, in most cases, two members of staff with some experience and training in profiling. During this year profiling developed tentatively in most schools with the exception of the school which had appointed a member of staff to deal with TVEI profiling and its development. The INSET work that this teacher did in this year is responsible for the robust state of profiling in that school. In other schools the process could be considered volatile in the extreme.

Evaluation should not be considered to be a threatening process, but several year tutors admitted that when they learned that the evaluators were to visit to see how the profiling process was developing they read the students' diaries for the first time. There was also a good deal of inertia amongst staff not directly involved in TVEI to participate in the cross-curricular profiling. This aspect of the profile was student initiated and apathy by some staff or direct refusal led many students to give up.

Where perhaps the best profiling was taking place and where the most intensive INSET was going on was in the subject specific profile. The general format of the profile was common to all schools but the manner of implementation was left up to individual schools and teachers. At the end of a module or section there would be a review of what had been learned. The content of the learning was either given by the teacher or in some cases negotiated between the teacher and students. The students then rated themselves on a 4-point scale. This scale had no criteria attached to it but there seemed to be a remarkable level of consensus as to what a 3 or a 4 meant. Having rated themselves the students then made a general statement about themselves. The teachers then confirmed or questioned the rating and made their own comments. An agreed statement about future targets was then entered on the pro forma. There was very good evidence from these forms, from observation and from interviews with students that real negotiation was taking place and most importantly that the students appreciated being actively involved in the assessment of their own progress.

Profiling in the subject specific area was the area of greatest advancement in the second year of the pilot. There are several reasons for this: although the pro forma was centrally devised, its implementation was local, thus individual subject teachers had ownership of the profile. There was clearly, as a result of the profiling process, a change in the relationship between teachers and students that was recognised by both and was of benefit to both. The feedback for the teacher was of equal importance to the student. After a short initial period of smarting, teachers reported that they benefited from being told that what was perhaps their favourite topic was boring.

The second year of the pilot coincided with the second year of the introduction of GCSE. At that stage few teachers were considering integrating their subject specific profiling with their continuous assessment of course work for GCSE. The possibility was recognised and there was an appreciation of how such an integration could alleviate some of the time problems.

When comparing the development of two of the components of the profiling scheme the contrast between the subject specific and the cross-curricular profiles was stark. This represents as much as anything the different prestige that teachers and students accord to 'subjects' as opposed to the pastoral side of school life.

Complexity and Ownership

The complexity of the scheme has been commented upon as has the ownership of subject specific profiles. In the third year of the pilot and the second year of operating the profiling scheme, how are schools dealing with the question of time? The authority has groups of schools in their first year of the extension with another group entering next year. All schools within the pilot are looking towards extension and wishing to widen the experience of all pupils. The development of profiling in the pilot was conducted by a small group of interested teachers on a small number of pupils and the critical factor was seen to be time. How much more important will the time factor be in extended profiling? Will extending profiling across the school also mean a dilution of the ideal process?

At the time of writing it is fair to say that the answers to these questions are not encouraging. In the school which has the most robust profiling scheme and the most successful INSET programme there have been important moves. In the summer a writing team amplified some of the cross-curricular skills on the CGLI 365 type scheme so that they resemble a self-assessment sheet on key study skills. Topics so expanded include Speaking and Listening, Writing and Reading, etc. The pro formas that have been developed guide the student through aspects of these skills and allow them to comment on their progress in them or even if they have had the opportunity to demonstrate that skill. Although there is a space on the sheet for the tutor to sign there is no indication that there will be any negotiation in the assessment, an essential part of the profiling process. Both the teachers and the evaluators fear that this scheme may in practice be reduced to a paper exercise because of the pressure on time. There is clearly dilution here.

In another school no changes have been made to the original scheme and attempts are being made to keep the scheme going. There is, however, insufficient time to carry out the profiling in either P.S.E. or in lessons and therefore it is done at lunch time. There is very little negotiation, more of an intermittent support scheme rather than profiling as such. That is, it is still a bolted-on activity and not accommodated into the mainstream of the students educational experience. Profiling, is here, on the back-burner.

In the third school considered here the profiling was done in the previous year almost exclusively by the TVEI co-ordinator. The intention this year was for that practice to continue. However, the LEA is about to issue guidelines for an authority-wide profiling scheme and the school awaits the imminent arrival of this document. We are all awaiting direction from the DES on profiling and records of achievement. This third school may be condemned for doing nothing at this moment but may well prove to be taking the wisest course in the long run.

The evidence from this evaluation is that the greater degree of ownership of the profile by the school and by individual teachers, the nearer the process is to the ideal state. It is questionable therefore whether national or local guidelines will have much effect on the one to one relationship between teacher and pupil.

10 Learning from unwelcome data: Lessons from the TVEI examination results

CAROL FITZ-GIBBON
School of Education, University of Newcastle Upon Tyne

Reactions to Data

Following release of data on examination results of TVEI and non-TVEI pupils (Fitz-Gibbon, Hazelwood, Tymms & McCabe, 1988), the team had some problems to face. There were some negative reactions which were disturbing, although understandable, and we must try to learn from them. Matters were not helped by exaggeration and selective reporting in *The Independent*. Nevertheless, the publicity given to the data can be defended, it will be argued here, on the grounds of defending the long-term interests of education by promoting the better use of social science. This article will be primarily concerned with putting forward the following arguments with that purpose in view:

1. As we repeatedly emphasised, *there was no firm proof that TVEI caused the lower examination performance.*
2. *The data should be regarded as formative and informative.* The pilot projects are not over and the appropriate response, in the best TVEI fashion, is to treat the information as a springboard for problem-solving.
3. *There are lessons to be learned from this TVEI experience for two of the next innovations which schools must take on board, namely performance indicators and target setting.*

Before developing these arguments it might be as well to review some of the points made in the article which reported the findings.

The possible explanations we suggested were: initial differences between TVEI and non-TVEI pupils; the fact that the data were intermediate not final results (the 2nd year of a 4 year pilot); the dispute during TVEI's implementation (teachers' 'action'); the time lost from the classroom; and the possible inappropriateness of the examinations for demonstrating what TVEI pupils had learned. No one can say for sure which explanations were valid; no one actually knows how much each factor contributed. The data must be treated as scientific information, needing careful interpretation, not as a summative judgement on even the one aspect of TVEI represented by examination results.

TVEI Did Not Necessarily Cause the Lower Examination Results

The problem here is the word 'cause'. TVEI pupils did get lower examination results than non-TVEI pupils and it is fairly safe to assert that this was a national pattern. But the very consistency in the data, nationally and locally, suggested that despite the variety of ways in which TVEI was implemented some factor present in practically all projects led to worse examination results. A prime candidate for that factor must be initial differences in pupils. This is the case because we know from a good deal of other research that differences which schooling makes are generally small when compared with the differences you find between pupils (e.g. Willms, 1987). If we pursue this possible explanation a little further we might ask in what ways TVEI pupils were different. The TVEI Operating Manual advised that the programme was for pupils 'across the ability range' and we found, indeed, (as did the MSC) that TVEI and non-TVEI pupils were about the same in average ability. The range of ability was less in TVEI however: there were fewer 'non-exam' pupils and fewer 'high fliers'. We applied statistical corrections for differences in ability and also ran a comparison between groups matched for ability, to eliminate the difference in range. The discrepancies remained. There were fewer girls in TVEI despite praiseworthy efforts to avoid sex stereotyping. Since girls get rather higher grades at age 16 we re-examined the data for boys only. Once again the differences remained.

Because of the large amount of information we had collected, we *were* eventually able to find a way in which TVEI pupils were measurably different from non-TVEI pupils. Peter Tymms invented a scale based on responses to questions about what pupils expected to do in the future, a scale called the Likelihood of Staying in Education measure (LSE). When questioned at the beginning of the project, in their fourth year, TVEI pupils were less inclined to stay in education beyond the age of 16 than were non-TVEI pupils. The LSE measure was quite strongly correlated with achievement (about 0.55) so, as we had done with ability, we made the usual statistical corrections for this difference, but still the examination discrepancy remained.

However, it is important to note that statistical corrections cannot fully compensate for initial differences. (Statisticians tend not to give this point the emphasis it deserves. It is indeed a problem which it is tempting to neglect since it arises in all survey work and there is a good and steady supply of such work. The only data in which the need for statistical 'corrections' does not arise is experimental data and there is a great dearth of that.)

In addition to the difference in attitudes to staying on at school, TVEI volunteers must have differed from non-TVEI pupils in other ways which we have not measured. *In summary, since TVEI was given to a group which was different to start with, the interpretation of differences at the end is very difficult*. Given that the results were not what one would expect or hope for, after the substantial resources and dedicated human efforts that had gone into TVEI programmes, we hope that this point will be widely accepted.

This problem of interpretation is very serious and is one which confronts other investigations, such as the trial of a new drug or of a particular cancer treatment. In other words it is a problem which is confronted all the time in medical research. Education and medicine both deal with human beings, each of which is unique and all groups of which are very variable in their responses. The solution adopted in medicine is the clinical trial or randomised experiment. In social science we shall have to use the same approach if we want to obtain clear evidence of the effects of various programmes. To present that argument in full would take at least another paper but suffice it to say that there have been controlled experiments in Education and more are needed (Campbell & Stanley, 1966).

The Exam Data should be Regarded as Formative and Informative

Apart form the initial differences explanation just discussed, which related to the kind of pupils attracted to take TVEI, other possible explanatory factors related to the way TVEI operated.

There was considerable agreement that there was too much absence from the classroom. Money may have been available to buy in supply teachers but in some schools they were often unobtainable, and in most schools it is almost impossible to get supply teachers qualified in important TVEI subjects such as business studies or information technology. And almost always a supply teacher will not get through the activities and work which the normal teacher would get through. We warned of this problem on the basis of interviews with pupils months before we saw any examination data. For those running projects the problem of supply teachers provides something to consider in planning inservice. For evaluators it suggests we should try to monitor absence from the classroom and see if it correlates with worsened examination scores.

Once again, however, the situation is not as simple as some would suggest. The time-in-the-classroom hypothesis needs careful exploration. The notion that time is a very influential variable in school achievement was strongly argued on the basis of some data from Detroit (Wiley, 1973) but was quickly refuted in a wider study of several cities (Karweit, 1976). Since the data for both studies was survey data, not based on experiments, causal relationships could not be assumed. The debate continues (Karweit, 1985). Time is a peculiarly flexible factor when considered as an input to teaching. Tasks can expand to fill the time available and many can also be hurried to fit the time available. It is regrettable but, due to the lack of experimental data we just do not know the extent of the influence of time lost from the classroom; we do not even know with any acceptable degree of certainty whether that was a factor at all . . . and nor does anyone else. This is not to say that individual teachers might not have a pretty good hunch for their particular case. They have access to enormous amounts of first hand information and may well be able to make judgements about their own particular projects. But for the large scale national pattern of data we do not have clear-cut simple explanations. As far as the time-lost-from-the-classroom hypothesis is concerned the examination data simply highlighted a problem which was already of concern.

Whilst there was no way to check the time-lost-from-the-classroom hypothesis except in impressionistic and qualitative data, there were some hypotheses which *could* be checked against the data. Writing in the newsletter of the Secondary Examinations Council (Summer 1988, no 9) the Director of MSC's Education Programme, asked if 'flexibility' (the inclusion of work experience, enterprise etc.) could only be gained at the expense of quality. 'Critics may argue . . .' she wrote, that the additions to the curriculum 'merely mean less time for real "subjects"; a difficulty which the more able students may surmount, but which may leave the less able with fewer qualifications than they would have gained under a traditional curriculum.' The hypothesis put forward here was that we would find less difference between the more able TVEI and non-TVEI pupils than between less able TVEI and non-TVEI pupils. This was a highly plausible hypothesis and because of its plausibility it probably seemed to many readers to be an explanation. This was unfortunate and demonstrates the need for a more cautious and scientific approach to data. Before publishing hypotheses in anything but a most tentative fashion, the data should be checked to see if there was any support for the hypothesis. The data readily available to the MSC had individual, pupil-level data for TVEI pupils, but unfortunately had only aggregated distributions of ability categories for non-TVEI pupils. Thus a breakdown by ability of the examination results was not possible. However, we had much better data: pupil level for both TVEI and non-TVEI pupils, a measure of ability rather than a teacher estimate, and data collected by ourselves under standardised conditions. We would have provided the necessary analysis had we known that it was wanted and we do so below (see Table 10.1).

In our data the hypothesis is not supported; in fact quite the reverse appeared to be the case. Plausibility is not everything.

TABLE 10.1 *Examination results broken down by ability groups (raw residuals after controlling for ability)*

Ability quartiles	*Examination Total Score*			*Grade Point Average*		
	TVEI	*Non-TVEI*	*Level of signif.*	*TVEI*	*Non-TVEI*	*Level of signif.*
Low 1	–0.8	0.2	0.20	–0.4	0.01	0.60
2	–2.8	0.8	<0.001	–0.21	0.06	0.001
3	–2.5	0.7	0.001	–0.21	0.06	0.002
High 4	–4.2	1.0	<0.001	–0.13	0.03	0.07

It was the least able pupils whose examination results were the most like those of similar pupils not in TVEI. The situation for more able pupils was more complicated. If one looked at total points scored in examinations (a kind of UCCA scale for examinations at 16 counting 7 for an A, 6 for a

B, 5 for a C or a CSE grade 1 etc.) then the more able *apparently* suffered most from participation in TVEI: they had a difference of 5.2 points on average, equivalent to getting 5 lower grades on the same number of examinations or getting one less examination at grade C O-level. However, if we look at the average grade achieved in whatever examinations were taken, it was the middle ability range which showed the greatest discrepancy, a quarter of a grade lower on average.

What conclusions can we draw from this further exploration of the data? The high ability pupils showed the greatest discrepancy on the sum-of-points scale, the 'examination total score'. They did not show the same amount of discrepancy on grades achieved. This suggests that if higher ability pupils suffered from being in TVEI it was because they were entered for fewer examinations. This is useful formative information and points to one way forward towards removing the examination discrepancy: be sure to enter bright TVEI pupils for just as many examinations as bright non-TVEI pupils.

Perhaps this exploration of the data can be used to reinforce the point about social science. It is not a good idea to throw out plausible hypotheses without trying to get some data to check them against. People should have been demanding good data on examinations not speculating. That is what 'careful monitoring', which the Operating Manual so properly called for, is about: replacing speculation with evidence. Which brings us to the final point about performance indicators and target setting.

Learning about Performance Indicators and Target Setting

As schools obtain their own budgets, the work of LEAs is to become increasingly devoted to 'setting goals and monitoring' (Cooper & Lybrand, 1988) and already they are being asked to think of simple numerical measures . . . performance indicators . . . which will assist this monitoring. It is suggested in documents from the Department of Education and Science that some at least of these indicators should be published (DES, 1988).

The yearly collection of Performance Indicators is a welcome move toward regular, careful monitoring and we fully share the hope and even expectation that such monitoring could improve education. Nevertheless, there would seem to be some danger in these developments which the problems with the TVEI examination data illustrate well. *Simple numerical facts are very difficult to interpret*. It would not be ethical to hold schools accountable for Performance Indicators which cannot be interpreted. The examination discrepancy between TVEI and non-TVEI pupils was a kind of Performance Indicator for TVEI. The simple interpretation was that huge sums of money had been spent (e.g. £400,000 per year targeted on 250 pupils) and the first stated and most measurable objective had not only not been reached but there even appeared to be negative effectiveness. Crudely interpreted that doesn't look like value for money. But we hope that the preceding discussion has shown how difficult the interpretation of a single set of data is. We urge that the TVEI Performance Indicators be viewed as formative information and we would urge that Performance Indicators (PIs) for individual schools should be viewed in the same light, at least until we understand much more about the amount of influence that schools can and cannot have on pupils' achievements and attitudes (Hazelwood *et al.*, 1988).

There are other reasons for concern. The DES is promoting the idea that PIs should be as simple and as few as possible (DES, 1988). That may sound attractive but it is, in fact, dangerous. Schools are complex and it is highly unlikely that they can be understood with a few simple indicators. Take the TVEI example again. If we hadn't measured a large number of variables (indicators) including pupils' attitudes to staying on in school, we would not have had any evidence to support our assertion that TVEI pupils were different from non-TVEI pupils. Rather than a few, simple indicators, what we need is a system of indicators which provides us with useful information for running schools and understanding how schools might achieve goals which are set for them. We need to measure all the factors which may possibly affect the goals that we are trying to achieve. The year by year data which national monitoring will provide might possibly be useful but it will in no way be sufficient as the cognitive outcomes of schools are not the only outcomes of concern . . . and they may not be the outcomes over which schools have most control. It may be necessary to set out, as we did in monitoring TVEI, to obtain high quality data on a large number of variables. Hoping that a computer network will spew out enough Performance Indicators to enable us to understand and improve schooling could be very dangerous. Monitors of systems need to be more pro-active and need to work from tentative models of how the system operates and achieves its goals.

Which brings us to the question of target setting. Again, schools are going to be asked to set targets. What sort of targets? How are they to be set? Are there good examples from our elders and betters?

The MSC set a simple target . . . TVEI pupils would obtain 'more' vocational qualifications. Maybe that simple target will be reached by the end of the four year pilot but the fact that despite relatively generous resourcing the target was not reached in two years must not be forgotten. Education is not a trivial pursuit although many without direct responsibility feel that educational solutions are obvious. They |are| as obvious, perhaps, as the location of the end of the rainbow. Solutions must be searched for with the information and rigorous methods and logic available from social science. Intuitions and hypotheses must be constantly checked. We might also point out that there was probably, and understandably, no great keenness to have progress (or lack of it) published for all to see. Should schools be subject to the publication of data which is also best viewed as interim and formative?

Are there more encouraging examples of target setting from elsewhere? The DES continues to propagate the following target:

> to raise pupil performance at all levels of ability so as to bring 80–90 per cent of all 16 year olds to the level of attainment expected and achieved by pupils of average ability . . . and to do so in a number of subjects. (Cited in a paper from the DES delivered at a conference on Performance Indicators, June 1988)

Where is the justification for such a target? What kind of upward shift in performance can reasonably be expected? There are answers to such questions now, due to the advent of meta analysis. Many intensive small scale interventions produce shifts of about 0.30 of a standard deviation, i.e. the effect size is 0.3. An effect size of 0.8 is considered large and occurs rarely in the literature. The target proposed translates into an Effect Size of 1.00, quite a phenomenal shift! What level of resourcing, what radical measures, are going to produce such a shift? The paper goes on 'To add precision to the objective for illustration the number of subjects has been taken as five'. Never mind the precision, where is the realism?

Our elders and betters show symptoms of having no sense of the amount of change which can be expected in an education system. This is disturbing.

A Final Point

It cannot be emphasised too strongly that the activity of monitoring examination results should *not* be taken as implying that they are the only aspect of concern. The monitoring was, indeed, only a small part of the evaluation activities undertaken by the team at the Curriculum Evaluation and Management Centre, Newcastle University. When a journalist wrote, to our annoyance and amazement, that 'none of the aims of TVEI have been achieved' he was indulging in exaggeration and over-generalisation and was, in *fact* not aware of the stated aims of TVEI. He was NOT quoting us.

Whilst researchers must press for widely collected, representative data for monitoring, and for the implementation of randomised controlled trials, the importance of experiences and anecdotes in deriving *goals* and clarifying *values* is not to be neglected:

> Sean aged 17 was overheard talking to friends: 'I was no good at anything at school' he said. Now there are some pupils who are not, relative to others, good at much, just as there are pupils who are good at everything. (There appears to be a very unfair distribution of talents in the world.) But Sean was not one such pupil. He played a mean set of drums, well enough to be hired in 'gigs'. He could run his father's business for weeks on end, responsibly. Perhaps the school didn't know these things but surely they saw the pleasant, kind, friendly, popular student other people saw. Apparently they never told him that he had very good inter-personal skills and he left school feeling he was 'no good at anything.'

Personally I think Sean would have been better off in a TVEI programme, with profiling, with practical skills appreciated and with value placed on more than examinations.

Sean's years in school feeling 'no good at anything' might actually have been damaging to Sean, and potentially, via thousands of disaffected Seans, to society. Perhaps TVEI began to alter school for pupils like Sean. What a pity TVEI was not implemented as a controlled experiment so that the short and long-term benefits might have had a chance of being proved instead of simply hypothesised.

We simply won't know until we do social science better.

References

Campbell, D. T. and Stanley, J. C. 1966, *Experimental and Quasi-Experimental Designs for Research*. Chicago: Rand McNally.

Coopers and Lybrand 1988, *Local Management of Schools*. London: HMSO.

DES 1988, Performance indicators for secondary schools: Some practical considerations. A discussion paper presented at 'Quality in Schools: A Briefing Conference.' NFER 29th June 1988.

Fitz-Gibbon, C. T., Hazelwood, R. D., Tymms, P. B. & McCabe, J. J. C. 1988, Performance indicators and the TVEI pilot. *Evaluation and Research in Education* 2(3), 49–60.

Hazelwood, R.D., Fitz-Gibbon, C.T. & McCabe, J.J.C. 1988, Student perception of teaching and learning styles in TVEI. *Evaluation and Research in Education* 2(3), 61–8.

Karweit, N. 1976, A reanalysis of the effect of quantity of schooling on achievement. *Sociology of Education* 49, 236–46.

— 1985, Should we lengthen the school term? *Educational Researcher* 14(6), 9–14.

Wiley, D. E. 1973, Another hour, another day: Quantity of schooling, a potent path for policy. University of Chicago: Studies of Educative Processes, Report No. 3. (Reprinted in M. Guttentag (ed.), *Evaluation Studies Review Annual*. Beverly Hills, California: Sage Publications. 1977.)

Willms, J. D. 1987, Differences between Scottish educational authorities in their examinations attainment. *Oxford Review of Education* 13(2), 211–32.

11 Some emerging issues in TVEI evaluation

DENIS GLEESON, MONICA McLEAN AND TREVOR SIGGERS
Centre for Social Research in Education, University of Keele

This chapter examines some of the main differences between evaluating TVEI as a Pilot [TVEI(P)] and TVEI as an Extension [TVEI(E)]. It is suggested that, to be effective, evaluators should be aware of both the methodological and political implications of investigating an initiative which is broad in scope and which sits uneasily alongside other central government initiatives. A principal argument is that evaluators need to position themselves to see how local management strategies and institutional practices realise and match the rhetoric of central policies and the anticipated outcomes envisaged by local education authorities. Of concern is the extent to which qualitative, formative and action-oriented evaluation can be tolerated by government or LEAs contracted to 'deliver' specific curriculum change via the imposition of national criteria.

From Pilot to Extension

The apparent differences between TVEI(P) and TVEI(E) are of scale and scope. Since 1983 TVEI has been able to draw on £250 million to fund LEA Pilot projects. These have tended to focus on a limited number of schools and colleges, and selected groups of students. In 1987 a further £900 million was allocated for a ten year extension period of TVEI. The aim has been to fund LEAs bidding for resources to provide curricular programmes which meet established TVEI criteria, including the notion of an 'entitlement curriculum' for all young people (14–19) in full time study. The slices of TVEI(E) funding are, however, proportionately thinner than those allocated for the student cohorts of TVEI(P) even though the required ingredients of this particular curriculum cake have remained constant. The reduction in the level of funding has not been accompanied by any lowering of expectations for TVEI as a means of bringing about curriculum development. TVEI in Extension still anticipates, through changes in the curriculum and teaching approaches, a more economically aware, technically capable, flexible, adaptable, and enterprising, future adult workforce.

The results of the evaluation of TVEI(P) were not available in time to inform the decision, in 1986, to introduce TVEI(E). Even had they been to hand it would have been inconceivable to envisage central government radically changing its policies, perhaps risking the impetus of its pre-determined legal and financial reforms of education. What is disturbing, however, is the way LEAs have been obliged to bid for scarce resources and to assume the role of a 'licensed agent' (Harland, 1987). They have, in consequence, found themselves adopting centralist strategies (despite the rhetoric of 'bottom-up' innovation), using targets, timescales, 'bottom-lines', and categorical-funding to 'deliver' curriculum innovation and change. The Education (no. 2) Act 1986, and the Education Reform Act 1988 have made LEAs increasingly sensitive to their status and to perceived criticism of their changing role, not least from critical evaluation which may be thought to put future TVEI funding in jeopardy. The potential contribution of formative evaluation to LEAs may, therefore, be subsumed within the imperative to secure funding and be seen as successful implementers of innovation.

The major issue that LEAs, schools, and colleges now face is one of responding to a variety of external demands and initiatives, of which TVEI is now but one. Yet, TVEI pre-dates GCSE, the National Curriculum and NCVQ, the Local Management of Schools (LMS), TRIST/GRIST and now LEATGS. While it is possible to see evidence of some of these later developments in the first TVEI(P) projects the pace of educational change has increased so dramatically as to overtake the initial impetus of TVEI. Certainly TVEI(E) must be seen in the context of these newer and often more influential developments. Indeed, it is demanded that Extension submissions must demonstrate how LEAs will respond to, and reflect, imminent statutory curriculum requirements including arrangements for National Curriculum and INSET provision. In the circumstances evaluators are unlikely to be able to attribute changes in teaching and learning solely to one factor: TVEI(E).

McCabe (1986a) suggests that TVEI evaluators are expected to 'bring simple order to a complex set of situations and variables'. Finding 'simple order' under TVEI(E) could, therefore, mean setting the initiative in the context of more explicit government policies for education, training and enterprise. The expectation of LEA-wide TVEI development, however, brings new situations and variables to bear which add to the complexity of the post-Pilot phase. The compactness of most Pilot projects has meant that evaluators could, over time, establish close relationships with individual institutions and teachers. It has been possible for a whole project to be managed as a case study. In such circumstances evaluation has developed the process of formative and action-oriented research within TVEI(P), which was by nature experimental and supportive of idiosyncratic innovation. The loose structures of TVEI(P) accommodated evaluation which has been able to generate internal debate. It has, for example, been able to question some of the central tenets and assumptions of TVEI, many of which figure centrally in the rhetoric and policy of Extension. Active learning and equal opportunities are two such examples. As curricular 'entitlements' they appear to be the 'right' things to prescribe, but for evaluators they still elude definition and test the imagination in finding evidence that they are being 'delivered'.

The implication of larger scale and more complex scope is, at its simplest, that the implementation and evaluation of TVEI(E) will be a more complex business. This presents evaluators with a number of inter-related political and methodological challenges. The methodological challenges are about how to encompass many perspectives, each demonstrating the interests and influences that formative evaluation can reveal. Broadening the perspectives or horizons, however, does not present evaluators with methodological difficulties alone. Here the political realm is entered. West (1978) points out that 'validity is an issue of focus and stance and not entirely methodology'. Two related factors are involved here. The first is, as West puts it:

> teachers and schools are at the other end of a very long arm that reaches all the way back to the engine room of politics.

The second is that if evaluators want to reflect on the reality of focused educational themes and issues, at the moment it is difficult to avoid commenting on the political debates, both national and local, which underpin current practice. Both factors have obvious implications which may take formative evaluation beyond its original brief, and maybe into conflict with sponsors at the local level.

Beyond the Brief?

The number of institutions and their geographical spread raises a number of methodological difficulties in devising evaluation strategies appropriate to large scale projects. Stronach (1986) advocates a number of principles of procedure for TVEI evaluators among which are: 'be seen'; ask key educational questions; try and understand 'what TVEI is like' and; be 'comparatively knowledgeable' about what is being investigated. These principles are most effectively adhered to by adopting qualitative, action-oriented, formative research methods which are characteristically small scale. Methodological difficulties may arise when there are many more institutions and people to see; when there is more to know about; and where national and local educational policies intersect. For example, since TVEI(E) developments are intended to affect all students (14–19) and the orientation of the whole curriculum, it is necessary for evaluators to be cognisant of the influence of other developments: the National Curriculum; the SEAC and its deliberations about GCSE, in particular those relating to modular courses and frameworks; WRNAFE provisions and NCVQ; the introduction of Records of Achievement; the initiatives of the education/industry lobby; and developments in the youth labour market. This means that evaluators must be aware not only of those curricular issues directly concerned with TVEI, but also of the role and influence of other groups with equally legitimate claims to an interest in promoting and/or supporting educational innovation. Included among such groups would be: non-TVEI teachers and senior management, LEA Inspectors, GRIST/LEATGS advisory teachers, school-based Professional Development Co-ordinators, Careers Officers, Education/Industry liaison staff, local employers and their various networks, and school consortia.

Where evaluators of TVEI(P) have taken a case study approach they have sought a view of what is happening based on the experiences and perceptions of the different groups involved. The task has been as Walker (1980) puts it:

> . . . to find ways of working where what we do fits to some extent the language norms and expectations of diverse groups'.

The methodological difficulties of evaluating an innovation on the scale of TVEI(E) might be addressed by adopting the procedures of 'condensed fieldwork' outlined by Walker. He suggests that such an approach can enable an in-depth, quickly reported portrayal of what is going on in schools, classrooms and LEA offices. He describes the approach like this:

> The notion of condensed fieldwork in part cuts us off from the

traditions of case study research in the social sciences and draws us closer to other traditions in journalism, documentary film making and the writing of biography. What we retain most strongly from social science is the attempt to be objective, impartial and well-informed.

Evaluators adopting 'condensed fieldwork' strategies in order to cover the territory must adhere to principles of procedure which avoid 'looking for angles', over-simplifying issues, and responding rather than reflecting on research data. Another consideration is that in attempting to design research schedules which provide timely accounts of what is going on at 'ground level', evaluators can miscalculate the receptivity of participants and/or sponsor to findings despite their being presented as supportive or qualified. At the institutional level evaluation may be perceived as a monitorial exercise for the benefit of the LEA and project management. At project and LEA levels it may be considered an impediment to the changes they are contractually obliged to implement in institutions which retain considerable powers of self-determination and control. From both these standpoints evaluation appears to hold a potentially uncomfortable but unique position of influence once access to local institutions, classrooms, meetings and working parties has been negotiated. By differentiating between 'reports from the evaluation' and 'evaluation reports' Jeffery (1986) has anticipated the increasingly sensitive relationship between the researcher and the researched in such categorically funded projects as TVEI(E). By using 'reports from the evaluation' the evaluator is able to offer perspectives on progress without seeming to pre-judge the process of initial development.

One lesson learned by TVEI(P) evaluators is not under estimating the importance of negotiating access and developing formative, professional relationships with teachers and senior management in schools and colleges. Bearing in mind the research issues of 'collusion' and/or 'collaboration' raised by Wragg (1984) such close contact of evaluation with practice provides the LEA sponsors with evidence on the current state of affairs which in the early stages of TVEI(E) may be considered threatening. The obligation placed upon LEAs to set aside at least 1% of their TVEI budget for evaluation does not always mean that they are willing sponsors of the exercise. The concern of evaluators to be effective is matched by LEA concerns not to be frustrated in the implementation of their programmes. The issues which begin to emerge focus on the distinctions to be made between the sponsor and the client/audience of the evaluation.

There has been a distinction made between democratic evaluation which insists on the principle of the 'right to know', and bureaucratic evaluation which justifies itself by 'the reality of power' (MacDonald, 1977). Evaluators of categorically funded projects need to steer a path between the two. They must negotiate with their sponsors, about what are and/or are not acceptable as interpretations, conclusions, and even predictions. In doing this formative and action-oriented evaluation requires the establishment of a quality of dialogue with its sponsors that will encourage open access to the field of enquiry. In this process there may be casualties: Simons (1984) records the termination of the evaluation of a categorically funded project because sponsor and evaluator could not agree about who had the right to say what about whom. The insistence that evaluators may be venturing 'beyond their brief' may become an increasingly common cause for sponsors' complaint as TVEI(E) progresses. The line of political sensitivity is likely to be drawn to a greater degree of fineness than happened in TVEI(P). In the interests of their democratic inclinations evaluators must recognise the place of diplomacy (Hewton, 1982), and the significance of literary style if they wish to aspire to 'best-seller' status (MacDonald, 1977). Evaluators may need to contest unwarranted control and be vigilant when their research is used selectively as a mechanism for legitimating practice and supporting claims for increased funding.

It can be anticipated that LEAs will become more sensitive to evaluation reports about their TVEI(E) developments. Kushner & MacDonald (1987) believe that as a curriculum innovation moves from its pilot stage and becomes extended into general practice a new inertia is generated on the part of its sponsors. The pragmatism of the original project is overtaken by a less flexible management of change with all the characteristics of a 'movement' rather than an enlarged experiment. The implication is that contract-bound LEAs are likely to be intolerant of any dissenting professional voice and the reservations offered by individual institutions. According to Kushner & MacDonald the danger is that there is:

> too much public legitimacy and rhetorical investment behind these developments not to go along with them.

The parallel danger for evaluators being that they:

> are largely co-opted into a conspiracy of pretence that the programmes are educationally and economically sound.

It might be the case, then, that TVEI(E) evaluators meet particular difficulty in negotiating with LEAs where, as a necessary part of their contract with the Training Agency, evaluation is employed under sufferance. From the point of view of the Training Agency, LEAs are middle management and as such can feel vulnerable. The local managers of TVEI(E) (in particular those at policy and executive levels) can, as Simons (1987) argues:

> find it threatening to reveal their allegiances, having to balance patronage from above with credibility from below.

Hopkins (1986) has suggested that evaluators may cease to be considered friendly if they raise issues relating to institutional motivation, student experience and staff development. In these circumstances it is not difficult for local power structures to create obstacles for evaluators who work under their 'patronage' (Hopkins, 1986 and Simons, 1987). There may also be repercussions at the classroom level of investigation. In conditions, for example, where an LEA feels threatened by revelations of inadequacy, teachers might also be more fearful of administrative disapproval and become more secretive with evaluators. With these possibilities in mind we return to the question of which perspectives are to be the focus of the evaluators' work.

Evaluation or Confirmation?

It is crucially important to agree through discussion with the 'sponsor' LEA what are 'fair and reasonable' conditions for the evaluation (Simons, 1984). These include agreements on what should be selected for investigation, and what methods are to be used. Formative and democratic evaluation should contribute to information which is useful for participants in making future decisions about action. However, what is 'useful' to one group of people might not be so to the next. Different groups within the hierarchical structure of LEAs, down through individual institutions to their students, parents and employers, will have different value systems, interests and responsibilities. Evaluators should feel in a position to observe and comment on process, as well as outcome, without favour to any one group, even though the reality of sponsorship may make notions of justice relative. It is methodologically and politically unsound 'to take the powerful participants more seriously and the others less' (Simons, 1987). Evaluators must keep faith with the confidences of such willing, but more vulnerable, participants as classroom teachers and their students, not least because the credibility of formative evaluation is based upon its access to and analysis of 'grass-roots' experience.

The pressure on LEAs to be seen as successful managers of centrally-funded initiatives may be reflected in the way evaluators tend to be guided towards examples of 'good' or 'interesting' practice. Successful innovations have great political value and their evaluation will undoubtedly be formative and action-oriented. What is equally important is why similar innovations in other schools and with other teachers seem able to achieve only moderate success, or become curriculum disaster areas, and consequently receive little encouragement on evaluation. It is almost as if there is a covert, and largely unintended institutional 'streaming' which is based on supporting innovative competence and performance. If such an observation holds water then the link between formative evaluation, replication, and dissemination of 'good practice' should be viewed with more scepticism. Alternatively, knowing why the curricular entitlement promoted by TVEI(E) may be difficult to implement in any uniform and comprehensive fashion could involve the evaluator in conveying conflicting messages about institutional morale, teacher attitudes, LEA and national policy itself. More importantly LEAs may feel obliged to either go through the motions of instituting remedial action, or shoot the messenger particularly if the messages threaten management and the basis of future funding. In contrast with the Pilot Project there is the real danger that evaluation under TVEI(E), notably at the level of institutional practice, may draw unwelcome attention to the general marginalisation and containment of TVEI rather than its integration and adoption within mainstream education (McCabe, 1986b and Gleeson, 1987, 1989).

While evaluation evidence to date indicates that teachers have identified with the aims of TVEI, they are usually at pains to say how closely it mirrors their own ideas of curriculum balance and relevance. Senior management and teachers acknowledge the contribution that TVEI resources have made to facilitate more realistic teaching and learning experiences for their students. However, a new realism is now beginning to occupy the attention of these very same heads and their staff, namely that the influence recently vested in the MSC/Training Agency has now been overtaken by an empowered DES. The National Curriculum, open enrolment, and LMS is the 'new' DES version of reality and, as such, may be considered unlikely catalysts for adventurous curriculum and organisational experimentation. The problem for evaluators is that TVEI(E) may be increasingly seen as an educational window-display: attractive and desirable but difficult to deliver in relation to the perceived constraints of the National Curriculum, NCVQ and other initiatives. Indeed, it may even be that given the current focus on performance and standards, TVEI(E) has elements which could appear too expensive to sustain or too broad to relate to a more prescribed curricular definition. Examples of this would be: enterprise; work-based learning; active learning; careers guidance; and community involvement.

How far then does the evaluator assume a broader brief, become tempted by a concern for the ultimate educational consumer interest, that of the student, and advocate TVEI(E) for its liberalising influence (if that is what it is doing)? The irony is that while TVEI(P) was at first subject to the criticism of teachers concerned about its potential divisiveness and vocationalism, its subsequent 'ownership' by practitioners has moved it towards a mixed, if not a truly cross-curricular, strategy. It may be that TVEI becomes a means by which schools can organise their delivery of the National Curriculum (Key Stage 4). Indeed, there is already some indication that a cross-curricular delivery of Core and Foundation subjects is becoming an acceptable strategy. In these circumstances the TVEI(E) evaluator could thus be faced with assuming a wider developmental role, in supporting more imaginative responses to TVEI(E) in the National Curriculum.

If such a view may be dismissed as conjecture and speculation, over and beyond the evaluator's 'brief', it nevertheless points to the changing context in which local evaluation takes place. However, what is indisputable is that, while the National Curriculum (and Records of Achievement) will be monitored by LEA inspectors/advisors and HMI, implementation will be the statutory obligation of individual maintained schools. On the other hand, the contractual obligation to implement TVEI(E) rests not with individual institutions but firmly with their LEAs. This arrangement implies payment on the assumption of results and, as such, not only gives TVEI its unique place in the history of education; it also creates the potential for tension between LEA project management teams and the schools, colleges, and teachers. Between these groups is the evaluator paid for by the keeper of the purse, the LEA, but expected by all to be fair to all. While the LEA expects the evaluator to report impartially on the progress of implementation, the reality of institutional performance may prove disappointing. The relationship between the LEA and its schools and colleges becomes analagous to the relationship between teacher and student: who is accountable for 'success' or 'failure'?

Direction Forward

Holly (1986) has advocated that evaluators should seek to be collaborative, illuminative, non-hierarchical, and foster critical dialogue with all groups. In order to proceed in this way with all groups it is important to make the distinction between being a 'tool of authority' (Simons, 1987) and having a sponsor. Scrupulous attention to maintaining a dialogue with the LEA and other involved groups will mean that evaluators are in a better position to stand firm when it is necessary. Simons goes on to warn against 'political docility' and exhorts evaluators to feel an:

> obligation to produce and make available public accounts of public programmes.

Such a sentiment, however, could imply that evaluation has a predominantly summative rather than formative role, and attribute greater credibility to the product than the process of innovation. Experiences within the TVEI(P) indicate that public accounts cannot wholly reflect, in the interest of confidentiality, the contribution external evaluation has been able to make in its support of individual institutions, their teachers, and also to project management teams. While it is important that the expectations and responsibilities of its summative role is appreciated, evaluation, as a predominantly formative developmental process, enables the progress of innovation to be placed in the contextual framework of current circumstance.

With the move from TVEI(P) to TVEI(E) there may be an increasing tendency for project management teams to become more structured and hierarchical as they increase in size. Related to the issue of funding discussed earlier may be moves towards greater bureaucratisation and the development of line management procedures which were unnecessary, inappropriate, or simply not affordable before. The style of TVEI(E) management and access to information become crucial issues when evaluation is concerned with establishing validity by triangulating its research perspectives. Where the relative openness of TVEI(P) becomes replaced by project management reticence, among the explanations to be anticipated will be the suggestion that in the early stages of TVEI(E) there can be little to evaluate: the project is 'finding its feet — do not disturb'. What is disturbing about this 'settling down' rationale, however, is that it discounts the process of ongoing critical review as a management strategy. 'Newness' does not provide immunity from mistakes; nevertheless, in terms of evaluation what is perceived as premature criticism is often unpalatable and can sour relationships. It is interesting how the encouragement of self-evaluation is more comfortably confined to the learning process of the students involved with TVEI.

One of the assumptions about hierarchical structures, at least by those in the upper echelons, is that there is a continuous flow of information upwards and effective direction downwards. The experience of evaluators questions such self-confidence and even suggests that it is the inability of educational management structures to control practice which often enables some teachers to be innovative and allows others to be ineffective. The picture suggested by Kushner & MacDonald (1987) that:

> TVEI is the pursuit of present plans of action rather than the exploration of alternatives

implies a confidence in the educational system which may be overrated. The experience of evaluation is that teachers often respond imaginatively and creatively to external demands, but the former would not have been realised without the interjection of the latter. If the truism holds that teachers are, in general, conservative they will respond, but they may not necessarily initiate change without a stimulus which is external to their classroom.

In the early days of TVEI(P) teachers were concerned about their freedom to develop the practices they wanted, and likewise evaluators about their freedom to report. Nevertheless, the invitation to claim substantial resources was not resisted and practitioners used them for their own purposes. The MSC was soon persuaded to modify its requirements in response to what was happening 'on the ground' (McCulloch, 1986 and Gleeson, 1989). The money was used for 'bottom-up', teacher-initiated experiments in cross-curricular courses, assessment procedures, and teaching and learning styles, which embodied what has become known as the 'TVEI philosophy'. As Jamieson (this volume, Chapter 14) points out the contract became a myth and LEAs revealed only what they thought was circumspect on MSC (now the Training Agency) Review Days.

The same subversion can be anticipated, and even welcomed, in the Extension phase of TVEI. However true to the contract LEAs may be, schools and colleges are, at one end of the spectrum, paying lip service to demands and implementing only what is least disruptive to their current practice and, at the other, transforming their curriculum programmes into what teachers think will be most beneficial for their students. Teachers are also addressing themselves to what might have been perceived as the contradictions between educational and vocational values. In TVEI(P), for example, teachers responded by creating modular programmes which use the experience of industry and commerce to enhance the learning of young people in group enterprises, and by relating careers guidance programmes to students' work-experiences. To a considerable extent the same still holds true for TVEI(E): teachers will continue to make local settlements because the prescribed targets of TVEI remain dressed in general statements. Such diversity of practice takes place within what Blackman (1987) calls 'spaces' between contradictions:

> Spaces are social sites created by the opposition of contradictions which allow the possibility to legitimate and validate other or alternative ideas.

The picture at the moment, then, is one of confusion, contradiction and uncertainty. This is inevitable when the system is in the throes of implementing a by-no-means universally applauded Education Reform Act (1988). Those involved with the implementation of TVEI(E) — development officers, advisory teachers, co-ordinators, LEAs, heads and principals, teachers, and evaluators — are beginning to grapple with what 'The Extension' means. Developments with a TVEI label will eventually become subsumed into the rest of the curriculum, but in the meantime it is unclear how this 'sea change' will come about. However, creative and worthwhile solutions can, as Blackman argues, arise from coping and acting on the disorder. As Raffe (1988) has commented:

> TVEI principles have run against the grain of the British Education system and, perhaps more importantly, of the British labour market . . . and therefore represent a test case of the structural constraints upon change in the Education System.

We should, therefore, keep in mind that TVEI(E) initiatives are only part of an attempt to make great changes in the British Education system as a whole. As evaluators we need to position ourselves in order to watch and report on what happens 'on the ground', in the spaces and in between the contradictions of current educational policy.

Note

1. The views expressed in this chapter are the personal views of the authors and do not necessarily reflect those of the Centre for Social Research, University of Keele.

References

BLACKMAN, S. J. 1987, The labour market in school: New vocationalism and issues of socially ascribed discrimination. In P. BROWN & D. N.

ASHTON (eds), *Education, Unemployment and Labour Markets*. Lewes: Falmer Press.

GLEESON, D. (ed.) 1987, *TVEI and Secondary Education: A Critical Appraisal*, Milton Keynes: Open University Press.

— 1989, *The Paradox of Training: Making Progress out of Crisis*. Milton Keynes: Open University Press.

HARLAND, J. 1987 The TVEI experience: Issues of control, response and the professional role of teachers, In D. GLEESON (ed.) *TVEI and Secondary Education: A Critical Appraisal*. Milton Keynes: Open University Press.

HEWTON, E. 1982, *Rethinking Educational Change — A Case for Diplomacy*. Guildford: The Society for Research into Higher Education.

HOLLY, P. 1986, Developing a 'professional evaluation'. *Cambridge Journal of Education*, 16 (2).

HOPKINS, D. (ed.) 1986, *Evaluating TVEI: Some Methodological Issues*. Cambridge: Cambridge Institute of Education.

JEFFERY, D. 1986, 'Professional evaluation: Sheep in wolf's clothing?' *Cambridge Journal of Education* 16 (2).

KUSHNER, S. & MACDONALD, B. 1987, The limitations of programme evaluation. In R.MURPHY & H.TORRANCE (eds), *Evaluating Education: Issues and Methods*. London: Harper & Row/Open University Press.

MACDONALD, B. 1977, A political classification of evaluation studies. In D. HAMILTON *et al.* (eds), *Beyond the Numbers Game*. London: Macmillan Educational.

MACCABE, C. 1986a, How to choose your evaluator. In D. HOPKINS (ed.), *Evaluating TVEI: Some Methodological Issues*. Cambridge: Cambridge Institute of Education.

— (ed.) 1986b, *TVEI: The Organization of the Early Years*. Clevedon, Avon: Multilingual Matters/HMSO.

MCCULLOCH, G. 1986, Policy, politics and education: The Technical and Vocational Education Initiative. *Journal of Education Policy* 1 (1).

RAFFE, D. 1988, Review article. *British Journal of Education and Work* 2 (2).

SIMONS, H. 1984, 'Negotiating conditions for independent evaluators. In C. ADELMAN (ed.), *The Politics and Ethics of Evaluation*. Beckenham: Croom Helm.

— 1987, *Getting to Know Schools in a Democracy*. Lewes: Falmer Press.

STRONACH, I. 1986, Practical evaluation. In D. HOPKINS (ed.), *Evaluating TVEI: Some Methodological Issues*. Cambridge: Cambridge Institute of Education.

WALKER, R. 1980, The conduct of educational case studies: Ethics, theory and procedures. In W. DOCKERELL & D. HAMILTON (eds), *Rethinking Educational Research*. London: Hodder and Stoughton.

WEST, R. 1978, The politics of evaluation: Stance, focus and methodology. In C. RICHARDS (ed.), *Power and the Curriculum: Issues in Curriculum Studies*. Driffield: Nafferton Books.

WRAGG, E. 1984, Evaluating TVEI programmes. *Perspectives*, 14. Exeter: University of Exeter School of Education.

12 Financial lessons for the TVEI extension

PAMELA YOUNG
University of London Institute of Education

Interest in the topic of examining the TVEI financial allocations and their outcomes arose four years ago for the author as a local education authority evaluator when addressing 'soft' attitudinal issues. Evaluation of 'hard'/statistical and 'soft'/attitudinal issues through national and local projects has been a major feature of TVEI accountability. It has contributed to both theory and practice of evaluation within TVEI as well as other educational matters. In addition to this well publicised evaluation, the Training Agency and local TVEI Steering Groups have sought what might be termed an audit to look critically at the allocation of resources to meet the criteria for TVEI. Linked to this largely unnoticed part of the evaluation there is the legally required audit of funded projects.

Members of the Authority's TVEI Steering Group were asking 'value for money' questions that could not be satisfactorily answered by the evaluator. Evidence of 'value for money' was difficult to obtain for various reasons and reliance had to be placed on personal judgements about the impact of allocating financial resources in particular ways upon the TVEI students that might be discernible. It was possible, for example, to survey and report on parental attitude to the TVEI where their children were participating. For example the preparation for, experience of and utilisation afterwards of work experience and to provide useful insights into employers about the value to them and the student of work experience. It was also possible to comment on the 'value added' by the TVEI but not to conduct a more rigorous approach based on a 'needs' analysis where there is an assessment of the current situation linked to financial matters, a forecast of outcomes, and most importantly, the steps in between to realise the outcomes.

Traditionally, in this, as in many local education authorities, an historic approach had been taken to resource allocation, rather than a needs approach. Thus a researcher wanting to adopt a 'needs' analysis was blocked by the lack of data with which to begin. What, for example, were the transport costs to ensure that a cross institution set of 'tasters' (half-day experiences of a wide variety of courses) be effectively presented? The authority in question did not have sophisticated information that allowed an institutional break-down of costs, the Local Authority Financial Institution System (LAFIS) was geared to the Treasury Department's list of headings rather than individual school costs and, even then, did not look at its formulae for allocating resources from a needs point of view. This financial background prompted the questions: what criteria does an LEA use in order to allocate its TVEI resources? If the criteria are clear, how does the LEA monitor the outcomes it will have presumably agreed when deciding upon allocating the resources?

The opportunity in early 1987 to look at 'value for money' in education, unconnected with TVEI, awakened interest in these two questions, and prompted an extra curricular look at the financing of the TVEI. In addition, the publication of the TVEI 'Financial Feasibility Study' (1987) at much the same time, was an additional pointer in the direction of financial allocation. Before we turn to consider the TVEI 'Financial Feasibility Study' (1987), it is useful to examine the background to current practice for lessons to be learnt for the future. At the beginning of the scheme, the Training Agency (then MSC) gave each authority participating in the TVEI Pilot Programme funding for five academic years, which enabled them to have resources necessary to bring about change in technical and vocational education in their 'front line organisations' — schools and colleges. These resources were intended to defray the additional expenditure an LEA required to educate young people under the scheme.

TVEI was in many respects a new venture for the organisations connected; the Training Agency had not worked with local education authority schools before, but it did have prior experience of funding new education projects. Its earlier work with the Youth Opportunities Programme (YOP) and its successor the Youth Training Scheme (YTS) provided the basis for establishing the criteria governing TVEI and the operational procedures to be followed. For the further education colleges newly linked with TVEI, the TVEI Operating Manual was no surprise. For many of them, MSC funding for YOPs (later YTS) and other schemes were already a significant part of their work programmes, thus there was a ready acceptance on item part of the operational procedures.

For the schools, and the LEAs, or rather the officers not previously connected with the Training Agency, these ways of working represented a major departure not only in curricular terms but also with regard to financial management. It was only after an uncomfortable period spent in coming to terms with an unfamiliar way of financial working, that an acceptance of, and conformity to the Training Agency's style developed.

The financial experience derived from the first 14 Authorities implementing TVEI established a ceiling for future schemes, of £2 million over five academic years (six financial years). This additional funding, in terms of an Authority's total education budget was a small but welcome addition in a period of rate limitation, when decisions were made to cut expenditure in all sections of local education authority services. It enabled LEAs who made successful bids to promote curriculum developments within the TVEI remit they were already interested in. The TVEI literature is replete with examples of new and exciting initiatives. But some LEAs back away from the Training Agency's persistent requests for 'hard evidence' of progress in achieving targets through effective resource deployment. What is not clear from the many published sources is how various Authorities carried out their analysis of needs before drawing up their submission and then carrying them out. Local politics must have played a part in most situations, notably in the selection of participating institutions, but with the resource allocation largely distributed on historically derived data than a needs assessment of 'customer requirements. This historic approach made it difficult for a local evaluator to provide a VFM response to Steering Group members' questions.

A Problem

With the extension of TVEI to all Authorities and secondary schools and additional non-advanced further education colleges, within the next few years it becomes important that the matter of VFM 'audit' be addressed in order that there is information available about resource implications upon which to base future educational decisions. Already there is considerable evidence from both local and national evaluations of the different patterns of organisational and administrative arrangements, different curricular approaches and different subject areas. There is probably vested within these differences evidence that Authorities have augmented MSC resources with their own, but have not charged them to the TVEI project. The 'TVEI Finance Feasibility Study' (1987) uncovered evidence of supplementation by Authorities to the TVEI budget, but the extent was unknown as there were problems in accounting for these appropriately. This issue of hidden subsidy requires examination, particularly in the light of financial delegation to schools and the distinction drawn between the mandatory and discretionary elements of the formula required by the Secretary of State from each LEA by September 1989.

The New Scenario

Under the Education Reform Act of 1988, TVEI, along with Education Support Grants and the LEA Training Grants Scheme, became part of the mandatory element of the LEA's administration. As such there will be little opportunity for supplementation as in the past. In addition there will be a package of resources attached to each pupil that will have implications for individual school budgets and result in a much clearer idea of a school as a cost centre. Another 'unknown' at present is the number of schools who will 'opt out' taking with them their allocation of funding away from the Authority's total budget allocation for education.

MSC's Own Procedures

Quite apart from the new financial context within which TVEI and the Extension find themselves, there is the matter of MSC's own data. As the Study Team of the TVEI Financial Feasibility Study (1987) remarked, 'that much data collected by MSC is based upon a "subjective" analysis of expenditure on each project' (para. 6.4(b)), where the analysis is based on headings like staff salaries and so on, for the project as a whole. The Study Team also noted that MSC had attempted to analyse cost by subject area but had found it of limited value as it was not possible to distinguish project setting-up costs from on-going costs and from developmental costs. The Study Team went beyond highlighting the problems with MSC data to produce unit costs for a limited number of activities and to discuss the problems associated with obtaining meaningful unit costs to enable efficient, effective and economic use of resources to be made in TVEI.

Possibility for Future Financial Evaluation of TVEI Activities

The Study Team suggested that any future financial evaluation work be limited to comparative financial evaluation studies of a range of activities to MSC by their advisers as being good practice, which ought to be promulgated generally, and to build models of the likely total cost of replicating and extending activities (p.200). The cost of such an undertaking would be expensive in terms of staff time but there is now perhaps an opportunity to conduct such work. On one hand there is the guidance given to LEAs in Circular 7/88 in drawing up their Formula on a needs basis, and on the other Audit Commission's (1988) experience of conducting VFM audits in local government including education. Together, these two sources, could provide a basis for establishing a wider spectrum of unit costs than was obtainable in the admirable Feasibility Study.

References

AUDIT COMMISSION 1988, *Performance Review in Local Government: Action Guide*. London: HMSO.

DES 1988, *Local Management of Schools Circular 7/88*. London: DES.

TVEI UNIT 1987, *TVEI Finance Feasibility Study Report*. London: Training Agency.

13 TVEI: Evaluation, economic policy and ideology

PETER SENKER
*Science Policy Research Unit,
University of Sussex*

Introduction

A few years ago, an attempt to assess the economic implications of TVEI concluded that 'the TVEI by itself is unlikely to contribute substantially, even in the long run, to the solution of fundamental skill shortage problems which afflict Britain in this era of rapid technological change' (Senker, 1986). Subsequent events and analyses are reviewed below, and provide support for that general conclusion.

The paper suggested that it was necessary to clarify TVEI's aims more clearly 'so that relevant criteria can be developed as a basis for evaluation'. This need still persists, and, for reasons outlined below, is most unlikely to be met.

TVEI was introduced in a hurry, and its objectives were never clearly formulated (Moon & Richardson, 1984). In the absence of clear objectives, it is difficult to establish sound criteria for evaluation.

TVEI has been implemented on a local basis, ostensibly in accordance with overall national objectives. The process of implementation is extremely complex. Suffice it to say that the basic process is one by which locally prepared proposals are submitted to the Training Agency — the successor to the Manpower Services Commission which initiated TVEI. Teachers and local authorities were 'enticed' into TVEI by 'generous funding during a period of fiscal austerity and the use of techniques . . . such as competitive bidding and contractual relationships' (Finegold & Soskice, 1988).

Bids for funding are evaluated by the Training Agency and decisions made on which proposals to support. To an outsider, this process appears somewhat mysterious. It has sometimes been suggested by those directly involved — not entirely in jest, I suspect — that the inclusion of particular 'buzzwords' and phrases in proposals such as student centred learning, negotiated learning, experiential learning, work experience, school community links, learning by doing, monitor, audit, annual review, performance indicators and, more recently, coherence, has helped to get projects funded. Here it is sufficient to note that the Manpower Services Commission has had the power to decide which projects to fund, and that those bidding for funds have not been in a good position to put pressure on the MSC to define its objectives more clearly. There have been many developments and changes in the ways in which TVEI funding has actually been deployed since the programme's inception. But a major extension to the programme — TVEI(E) — has been introduced without any further clarification of national objectives.

Nevertheless, TVEI resources have often been put to good purpose. For example, an evaluation conducted in 26 schools concluded that schooling had become a more worthwhile and relevant experience for many students (Barnes *et al.*, 1987:168). Many TVEI lessons had been lively and interesting, students had been given more responsibility and their relationships with teachers had improved. But there were problems too: many teachers faced the need to accommodate rapidly to an initiative imposed on their schools. And many non-TVEI teachers and students resented the additional resources deployed on TVEI students and teachers.

Original National Objectives

TVEI can be seen as one element in the present government's education policy which aims to adapt education more closely to the needs of industry. The government's education policy can be seen in turn as forming part of an economic strategy designed to correct the long-established trend for the British economy to fail to progress as rapidly as other advanced industrial economies — in particular the British economy's failure to grow as fast as the economies of the United States, West Germany and Japan.

The essence of the Government's economic strategy can be summarised as follows:

1. The overriding aim of restraining inflation by means of monetary policy as the government's principal contribution to the reduction of unemployment.
2. The reduction of personal taxation in the attempt to give people the maximum incentive to strive for economic efficiency.
3. The destruction of trade union power which is percieved as having the effect of monopolising labour supply, thus promoting inflation and tending to reduce economic efficiency.
4. The transfer of as much of the economy as possible into the private sector with the intention of subjecting it to market forces. It is believed that this will stimulate efficiency.
5. The use of the education system to provide a labour force educated and motivated to provide the raw material for more rapid economic expansion.

This provides a context in which to consider the government's education policy — including both the National Curriculum and TVEI.

At the time that TVEI was initiated, a major objective was to increase the relevance of education to the subsequent careers of those who undertake TVEI courses. TVEI's aims were stated as specifically to 'open to young people within education, across the whole range of ability, a technical and vocational route to recognised national qualifications'. TVEI was designed to provide opportunities for school children to take technical and vocational courses combined with work experience. The government believed that this would enhance their employability and provide a workforce with more relevant skills.

It has been suggested that TVEI formed part of a strategy intended to ensure that skills and competences imparted in vocational education and training meet employers' needs much more closely. The development of up-to-date skills and 'flexibility' are required to cope with very rapid changes in technology and work organisation which need to take place in a modern competitive economy (Rees *et al.*, forthcoming).

Establishing Criteria for Policy Evaluation

In principle, the process of policy evaluation consists of examining the objectives of policies and deriving criteria for assessing whether policies are succeeding or failing. Having derived such criteria, the results of the policies are assessed and measured against the criteria to ascertain the extent to which the policy objectives have been achieved, and as a basis on which the policy can be improved.

The government has been successful in reducing trade union power, privatising large sections of industry, and reducing direct taxation. The extent to which these measures will have long-term beneficial effects on the economy is still by no means clear. Productivity has certainly been rising over recent years, but has not been matched by expansion of output: imports have been rising faster than exports, giving rise to enormous balance of payments deficits. Inflation has fallen, but is now rising again. Unemployment rose sharply at the beginning of the 1980s, has fallen substantially from peak levels, but is still high.

Evaluating the Government's economic strategy as a whole is difficult enough. Evaluating TVEI, which forms only a tiny part of it, is even more difficult, especially as, at least ostensibly, policies are designed to have long-term effects rather than to produce immediate benefits.

Matching Education to Industry's Needs

The government assumes that employers are best placed to judge their own present and future skills requirements: they should therefore be much more closely involved in determining the content of vocational education and training to ensure that schools and colleges deliver people with the relevant education and training. It has been suggested that government policies are based on the assumption that

> economically rational employers recruit workers to carry out rapidly changing work tasks on the basis of the degree to which these workers are able to demonstrate (often through formal qualifications) that they possess the appropriate technical skills, and the 'ideal worker' is conceived as someone who will adapt flexibly to the changes which will occur through his or her occupational career (Rees *et al.*, forthcoming).

Comparison with vocational training in the relatively successful West German economy could have provided the original rationale for TVEI. Prais (1981) has shown that only 30% of the British workforce have intermediate vocational qualifications such as apprenticeships and City and Guilds certificates, while double that proportion (60%) have comparable qualifications in West Germany. While West German vocational education and training may have been largely responsible for the post-World War II German 'economic miracle', it is far less certain that vocational education and training to national standards is the key to economic success in the present Information Technology era. In this era, the outstandingly successful country in economic terms has been Japan. And the Japanese school curriculum is broad and academic in character. After the compulsory school leaving age of 15, most Japanese stay on at school until 18, and at this stage, a substantial proportion do take technical courses.

Visiting Japan last year, we studied how small engineering companies were coping with new technology. We found that they recruited school leavers who had continued with their academic studies until 18 to train for technical jobs such as those which would normally be undertaken by craftsmen in Britain. They generally preferred to recruit people who had continued their academic studies until 18 in preference to those who had taken technical courses after leaving school at 15 (Senker, 1988).

In Britain:

> For many employers the most important criteria in selecting employees are not the technical competences which they have acquired through training or even previous work experience, but rather their social attributes . . . perhaps most crucially their characteristic attitudes towards work and their responsibilities towards their employer . . . Certainly, for example, it appears that Japanese firms investing in Britain — often taken as the exemplar for domestic companies — have been in the forefront in implementing recruitment practices . . . which are more concerned with identifying and consolidating appropriate attitudes — punctuality, reliability, commitment to the firm and so forth — than with selecting individuals with particular technical abilities (Rees *et al.*, forthcoming).

The recruitment practices operated by the Japanese companies in Britain reflect many aspects of their practices at home in Japan. The Institute of Manpower Studies (1984) concluded that major Japanese employers were not interested in recruits' vocational education: they recruit people at various levels on the basis of their attitudes and their general level of educational attainment. In Japan, the common core curriculum of seven compulsory subjects 'focusses unwaveringly on "the fundamentals" — including the three R's in our terms'. Japanese education does not include technical elements in school curricula up to the age of 16, and this 'failure' does not seem to have adversely affected economic performance.

The report suggests that Japanese employers seek people with ability to learn and to work with others. Similarly, Sako & Dore (1988) suggest that the

> lack of vocational education which is directly applicable (without further training) to jobs does not much worry Japanese employers. What they look for in recruitment and selection for long service is, first general intellectual ability as indicated by school record, and then, among those of the requisite ability, candidates with the right personality and attitudes as reflected by extra-curricular activities.

In such respects, Japanese and British companies appear to adopt broadly similar approaches.

Recent Developments

TVEI has changed in many ways since it was introduced. For many reasons, TVEI(E) differs markedly from TVEI which, in principle, was supposed to be its forerunner or 'pilot'. Not the least of the differences between TVEI(E) and TVEI have arisen because of the advent of the National Curriculum and GCSE — it is now often suggested that the aim of TVEI(E) as applied to 14–16 year olds is to provide a 'technological dimension' in the delivery of the National Curriculum leading to GCSE.

It would appear that the National Curriculum was introduced in the light of the perception that it might be the higher standards achieved by children of average ability in basic school subjects, in particular mathematics, in countries such as West Germany and Japan that could be critical for economic success (e.g. Prais, 1984).

Finegold & Soskice (1988) suggest that the whole of educational policy is in a state of some confusion. The authors criticise the government's education and training policy for its lack of coherence. For example, they suggest that one of TVEI's original objectives was to improve school staying-on rates. Subsequently, this has been soft-pedalled because TVEI's 16–18 phase comes into conflict with YTS. TVEI's efforts to bridge traditional subject boundaries are in danger of being undermined by the proposed National Curriculum which involves individual subject testing. An evaluation conducted in 26 schools suggests that it is unlikely that

> any real change will occur in the subject oriented, content dominated classroom behaviours that have characterised British education for so

long. The subject orientation of GCSE fits the organisation of schools and the ways that teachers have been trained, whereas some of the TVEI assessment developments pose severe challenges (Barnes *et al.*, 1987: 94).

Such contradictions can be traced to divisions within the Conservative Party. For example, there are those within the Party who wish to spread technical and vocational subjects across the comprehensive curriculum, and those who want to resurrect the tripartite system's technical school track by establishing City Technical Colleges.

Some Tentative Conclusions

It seems that trying to evaluate TVEI is a bit like trying to evaluate the effectiveness of a drug whose chemical composition changes over time and between different places, which has been prescribed on the basis of a wrong diagnosis with the aim of curing a condition other than that from which the patient is suffering.

The rationale behind TVEI appears to be essentially economic. Deficiencies in the education systems, demarcation problems in industry, strikes, and the failings of nationalised industries have all undoubtedly played some role in Britain's relative economic decline. But I contend that, if, indeed, a diagnosis of Britain's economic problems underpinned the original conception of TVEI, then that diagnosis was seriously flawed.

There is no space here to present a more coherent analysis of the reasons for the decline of the British economy relative to such countries as West Germany and Japan. My own view is that manufacturing industry employers' failure to invest enough in Research and Development and training, and their failures to modernise their production processes and products and to demand and train the people necessary to carry out these activities successfully would form key elements in such an analysis.

But these are national problems and many decisions on implementing and evaluating TVEI are taken locally. Nevertheless, one key question still remains unanswered: what criteria are used as a basis for funding decisions, whether on a national or a local basis?

Those bidding for funds, whether for education or for evaluation, may well believe that it is not in their best interests to press the Training Agency too hard to make its criteria more explicit. The Training Agency can reasonably hide behind the need to be flexible so as to meet local needs.

In the absence of clear objectives, the pervasive use of concepts such as 'auditing', 'monitoring', and 'performance review', is unlikely to contribute to the ostensible aims of increasing the efficiency with which resources are used. But it could well help to diffuse the ideology of market forces in the education system — and, perhaps, in the community at large.

TVEI, and its successor TVEI(E), offer resources to an education system short of resources. Perhaps more important, these initiatives offer resources for educational innovation. The available evidence indicates that the vast majority of those involved are concerned for the welfare of their pupils, and seek to use available funds as best they can, within the constraints placed on resource use by the Training Agency. Similarly, those who conduct evaluations may well carry out the best research of which they are capable, in order to obtain good data and make useful analyses.

I suggest, however, that the whole TVEI 'industry' — including both educational provision and evaluation — is built on unsound foundations. Although TVEI resources are often being put to good purpose, it is likely that they could be used better if they were distributed on a more rational basis — and not on the basis of an ill-thought out and hurriedly introduced initiative, which is developing incoherently in a rapidly changing environment.

Some of the possible ideological implications of TVEI/TVEI(E) have been alluded to briefly. Such considerations may also be relevant to evaluation. Given that many of us live off grants, and given that TVEI evaluation funding is quite substantial, some may feel that it could be wise to swallow any lingering doubts about the soundness of the whole TVEI/TVEI(E) enterprise.

It is suggested sometimes that the education system has 'domesticated' TVEI. Perhaps there has been domestication: but, if so, who are the dogs and who are the masters?

References

BARNES, D., JOHNSON, G., JORDAN, S., LAYTON, D., MEDWAY P. & YEOMANS, D. 1987, *A Second Report on the TVEI Curriculum*. University of Leeds School of Education.

FINEGOLD D. & SOSKICE, D. 1988, The failure of training in Britain: Analysis and prescription, *Oxford Review of Economic Policy*, 4(3) Autumn.

INSTITUTE OF MANPOWER STUDIES, 1984, *Competence and Competition*. London/Sheffield: National Economic Development Office/ Manpower Services Commission.

MOON, J. & RICHARDSON, J. 1984, Policy-making with a difference? The Technical and Vocational Education Initiative. *Public Administration* 62(1), 23–33.

PRAIS, S. J. 1981, Vocational qualifications of the labour force in Britain and Germany. *National Institute Economic Review* 98, November 47–59.

— 1984, What can we learn from the German system of education and vocational training? In G. D. N. WORSWICK (ed.), *Education and Economic Performance*. London: Gower, p. 47.

REES, G., WILLIAMSON, H. & WINCKLER, V. Forthcoming, The 'New Vocationalism': Further education and local labour markets. *Journal of Education Policy*.

SAKO, M. & DORE, R. 1988, Teaching or testing: The role of the state in Japan. *Oxford Review of Economic Policy* 4(3) Autumn.

SENKER, P. 1986, The Technical and Vocational Education Initiative and economic performance in the United Kingdom: An initial assessment. *Journal of Education Policy* 1(4), 293–303.

— 1988, Information technology and training in small engineering firms in Japan and England. An Interim Report prepared for the Engineering Industry Training Board, Science Policy Research Unit, University of Sussex.

14 Markets, rules and culture: TVEI and the management of change

IAN JAMIESON
School of Education,
University of Bath

Introduction

As the largest exercise in planned curriculum change since World War II, TVEI presents the theorist of change with a wonderful laboratory. And yet theorists of change are largely confined to the academy; their obfuscating language, their separation from the world of action, their reluctance to engage with practitioners in the construction of middle range theory, plus an Anglo-Saxon culture which derides theory — all these have traditionally insulated the university and college from the world of the practising bureaucrat, policy maker and teacher. It is true of course, that in recent years the 'teacher as researcher' movement working along the Cambridge–East Anglia axis has made some small inroads into the teachers' world. The world of the bureaucrat and policy maker has been more difficult to penetrate and yet it could be argued that theirs was the greatest need.

TVEI was born out of government frustration with the LEAs' resistance to change. Remember the difficulties that LEAs had in responding to Circular 14/77 where the DES asked them to supply details about their arrangements for the school curriculum. Many had only sketchy knowledge about what their schools were doing; LEA curriculum policies, where they existed, were superficial and prone to vague generalities. Even where there were clear cut policies it was a rare LEA which had either the will or the ability to make them stick in the schools.

Faced with the desire for radical curriculum change the government of Mrs Thatcher had one advantage over previous administrations. It did not feel bound by conventional wisdom, indeed one can find evidence to support the thesis that in many areas of public life, education included, it was positively anxious to tear up the post-war consensus and 'break the mould'. Those who wish to institute radical change have three incentives with which to work (Rodwin, 1984). They can use the market [money], they can use the law (administrative rules), or they can use moral exhortation (attempt to change the values and culture). In the area of curriculum change exhortation has been the traditional weapon of government, and LEAs and schools have been systematically deluged with advice and suggestions flowing from the DES and HMI. In a system awash with exhortation this had remarkably little effect.

The Market

Against this backdrop the government changed tack. Having systematically starved schools of resources it now used the incentive of money to persuade them to its will. Categorical funding, the bidding system, the Don Corleone model of curriculum development — call it what you will, it has had a profound effect on the whole education system, and of course it was pioneered by TVEI. The government, through the MSC, offered substantial sums of money in return for LEAs undertaking to 'deliver' a curriculum which met certain criteria laid down by government. The model managed to combine brilliantly the desire for the centre to control and shape developments, but at the same time to harness the energy and commitment of local ownership of locally drawn up plans. One of the most interesting questions is whether anybody in government conceived of this as a model of change or whether, like most things in political life, serendipity ruled. Although this model evolved from the centre it has had wide influence on management in the TVEI pilot projects. Consortia and individual schools have been asked to bid for TVEI monies in TVEI extension thus replicating the model at local level, and there are even cases of departments and faculties competing one with another inside institutions to deliver certain aspects of TVEI.

Rules: The Myth of the Contract

Central government has always given the LEAs money for education, some of it earmarked for specific priorities. Unfortunately local treasurers have often found more pressing local concerns and central government targets have been missed. TVEI was to be different, the LEAs were asked to sign a contract to deliver against their agreed bid and the contract was to be monitored and audited by the MSC.

The 'contract' is largely a myth, but like all myths it is both powerful and enduring. Locally it is based around the sacred book, the aptly named LEA submission. TVEI directors and co-ordinators regularly point to it and expect submission from recalcitrant headteachers and LEA officers ('we have to do it because it is in the submission — submit'). Like all sacred books it contains its own special language which is powerful but elusive. A good example is provided by the new litany of teaching and learning: student-centred, negotiated, criterion assessed, experiential, active etc.

The monitoring of the contract takes the form of the AAAs: Auditors, Advisers and Annual Review. MSC auditing is little different from any other, the accountants examine important trivia — important because it is necessary to have cost control and to ensure that things like the rules of virement have been followed, but trivial in the sense that it is a long way from teaching and learning. The annual review, where the massed ranks of MSC and DES officials meet the massed ranks of the local TVEI project, is unquestionably a home match as far as the local projects are concerned. Although billed as a mutual exchange of views, a forum where genuine difficulties might be exchanged, the institutional arrangements nearly always prevent this. There is too much information to digest in the form of the annual report, yet too little information on really crucial issues. The away players rarely seem to be able to find the really penetrating question. In fact the concept of the contract and its policing plus the institutional arrangements of a very large meeting with 'two sides' ranged on opposite sides of the room effectively determine the nature of the discourse. TVEI co-ordinators conveniently forget all they ever knew about room organisation and active learning — the bureaucrats never knew it in the first place. The home side field a defensive formation and the evaluator ('she who knows the truth') has been given her text from Joseph Heller, 'You're too important in your own right. And you'd be much more valuable to us as an independent voice in our control', (Heller, 1980). Whether the new (actually renewed) interest in performance indicators (remember the Newcastle Commission of 1862) will make any difference to this is an interesting question. The current near universal indicators of gender and ability spread clearly do put some pressure on projects to move in the approved direction. The difficulty is that as the indicators move into softer ground, e.g. process indicators, there is much more scope for 'interpretation' and 'adjustment'. The rules of discourse have had several practice runs of course through the projects' steering committees. Here too, the rules of conduct are clear. Leading members from industry and from the political parties know that the name of the game is *marketing*, they want to know whether the product is up to specification and whether it works. The notion of action learning pilots to test strategies and ideas is alien to them. And the idea of 'learning through failure' an absurdity that only the academy would dream up.

Such ideas are not wholly alien to the MSC advisers who are the front line troops for policing the contract. Theirs is a difficult role, not so far removed from the model of critical friend so beloved of the evaluation fraternity. Their difficulty is that there are too few of them, their territories are too large and they have too little time for the task. There are structural difficulties also — not only is their combined role of policeman and social worker inherently difficult (should they uphold the interests of the client or the rule of law?), but they have unclear instructions from Head Office. Is anybody now clear what TVEI is about — the current rhetoric of teaching and learning styles seems a long way from the Callaghan inspired technical and vocational revolution. Furthermore, the salary and conditions of service of such jobs do not appear to have attracted many who are capable of assuming the mantle of policy expert, management consultant, HMI and LEA adviser all rolled into one. The job is practically impossible for a head or deputy with limited experience of a few schools and a few LEAs.

Fighting Bureaucracy

Most TVEI co-ordinators understand the myth of the contract although they still use its power. They have discovered that even in TVEI extension, where the power of the market has declined significantly, the power of rules still holds sway. After all only they have had a really good look inside the gift horse's mouth and seen how few teeth it possesses. The world of rules and regulations, of auditors and due process is the world of the LEA bureaucracy.

We have heard too little in TVEI of the way in which the different sizes, characteristics and cultures of LEAs effect the way in which TVEI has been managed. We have been left with little more than ideal types which have been strung out along the centralised/proactive and decentralised/reactive continuum. Here the style and structure of the LEA seems to be congruent with certain management strategies and structures (and where it isn't major problems ensue). Centralised LEAs are more likely to have a TVEI blueprint which they attempt to impose on all the institutions via a strong central team often located in the LEA headquarters. By contrast the decentralised LEA adopts a more *laissez faire* approach and lets individual institutions run their own show within the broad TVEI criteria. Occupying the middle ground we have consortia where clusters of institutions deliver the programme. The consortium approach is itself influenced by LEA culture. In centralised LEAs the consortia are more likely to have evolved a system of shared timetabling and shared resources, a rational division of labour (the centres of excellence model), as well as a division of the spoils. The ultimate mark of this model is where teachers from one institution are teaching children from a second institution in a third institution. It takes a strong LEA to lower the boundaries of individual institutions and make this work. Towards the *laissez faire* end of this continuum the consortia are mere labels for the combined activities of individual schools and colleges. Quite how this crude analysis is complicated by factors like LEA size, political composition and rural-urban divisions we know not.

Although LEAs may differ one from another, from the TVEI co-ordinator's position they all have one thing in common — they are bureaucracies — organisations that run by a complex system of rules driven by the principle of due process and the committee cycle. This traditional mode of operation, which is marked by a relatively slow time response, grates hard against the sense of urgency generated by all the pilot projects. The projects have relatively large resources but short time spans, and they feel frustrated by the cumbersome decision making process of the LEA bureaucracy. Where these local projects have strong industrial representation these lieutenants of industry (the captains rarely serve), also express their bewilderment and displeasure at local government bureaucracy. There is more to this question than mere managerial impediment however; it represents an important clash of managerial cultures. On the one hand old style bureaucracy: marked by slow democratic decision-making, compromise, and clear goals and strategies. By contrast there is enterprise management: marked by rapid decision making, often using an action learning model (Revans, 1981) where goals and strategies are evolved 'on the hoof'.

The inevitable clash of these two philosophies makes managerial life difficult in TVEI. In the first place TVEI co-ordinators who have been plucked from the ranks of serving teachers find LEA bureaucracies difficult to fathom, particularly the large number of different departments and sections (finance, architect, minor works, staffing, FE branch, schools branch etc.) none of which appear to talk to each other! This can lead to dangerously stereotyped views — a remote, unfathomable bureaucracy out of touch with schools and colleges contrasted with a free spending, semi-autonomous project which seems intent on breaking, or at least bending, all the LEA rules. Various attempts are made to reduce this dissonance. Centralised authorities, where the watchword is control, often appoint an LEA officer or adviser to run the project, or the project's administrative centre is brought into the LEA headquarters. Less centralised authorities often appoint an LEA 'broker' to mediate between the two structures.

The crucial question is which model works best, where the criterion is effective learning? Before coming to a judgement we must remember that there is a general educational antipathy towards bureaucracy, educationalists in the educational change business believe that centre-periphery type models with strong centres do not work. The new orthodoxy gives power to the periphery, grows it from the bottom up and intones the karma of 'ownership'. Certainly this way you are more likely to harness the energy and commitment of teachers and pupils, but whether it will be wholly in the 'approved' direction is less certain. Surely the adoption of this model is the major cause of the 'domestication' of TVEI, the erection of student-centred teaching and learning styles as the major totem pole of the new faith.

Fighting Feudalism

In the bureaucratic fight the main weapons in use relate to administrative rules. The TVEI co-ordinators try to create a climate of enterprise and innovation within the regulatory framework of the LEA. However difficult the LEA bureaucracy is, the TVEI co-ordinator knows that the main battleground for change is in the schools and colleges. This is a classic war on two fronts — the kingdom may belong to the LEA but the major battle sites are under the firm control of the Barons (and occasionally Baronesses) in the institutions. They are old campaigners with a tradition in most authorities of relative autonomy and boundary maintenance. Initially the major weapon of change was monetary — the Barons were to be persuaded to give up some autonomy (over budgets, staffing, timetabling, curriculum) in return for resources. The change was to be made to stick by the use of rules (the contract) and efficient policing (audit and evaluation). Time was limited because of the extra resources and the external evaluation were there only for the duration of the pilot; in the end the innovation had to be sewn into the fabric of the school and held there by a set of structures and supporting values.

The success of this strategy is still difficult to gauge although some of the factors which induce change at this level are clear. Simple things like the amount of money and the efficiency and profile of the evaluation are important. More complex is the effect of factors like the positional and personal power of the TVEI co-ordinator and her/his understanding of change strategies (it is actually true — there is nothing so practical as a good theory). The role of headteacher is a curious one, occupancy of the role is like the membership of a club and ex-members of the club tend to recognise each other instinctively. Education also has a well developed sense of hierarchy. If we put these two factors together I think that there is sufficient evidence to support the hypothesis that co-ordinators who have not been heads, and/or who are not paid at comparable headteacher scales have credibility problems with the barons.

Inside the schools there are other forces at work. Some TVEI projects appointed external teachers to become institution co-ordinators, others went for internal appointments, many went for a mixture. There does not appear to be any clear evidence on what was the most successful strategy. The internal appointments obviously knew the ground better but were often hampered by old allegiances and old ideas. The newcomers often had a clearer idea of the necessary innovations but were hampered by their lack of institutional knowledge. Newcomers quickly realised that their long term future was likely to lie not with the temporary structures of the TVEI project but with their host institution.

One of the most important effects of TVEI inside institutions is to release new forces for change. TVEI has fostered the rise of the 'technological proletariat' — new empires are being forged in the white hot heat of the CDT forge. As Harland (1987) has noted, TVEI has given an opportunity for teachers of subjects which have traditionally been marginal to the mainstream curriculum — CDT, Business Studies, Home Economics, and entirely new areas like Information Technology — to rise in the school hierarchy.

Evaluation

External evaluation was something which the pilot TVEI projects rarely managed, certainly in the early years of the initiative. Many of the projects had external evaluation because the MSC insisted on it and they duly handed over their 1% to the evaluator — the 'expert' on the mystical yet 'scientific' craft of evaluation. There was very little discussion or negotiation on these evaluation contracts, certainly not on crucial questions like the appropriate evaluation model, or on the different roles the evaluator could play (consultant, trainer, auditor, honest broker etc.). Broadly speaking the LEAs and their TVEI projects failed to take on the role of client and treat the evaluator as a contractor.

The failure to manage produced some inevitable early difficulties. There was a degree of client dissatisfaction with both the ways in which evaluations were presented (there was often uncertainty and disagreement about the audience) and their usefulness. LEAs often preferred output orientated data that was quantifiable ('hard') and which was relevant to policy making. Academic evaluators, influenced by the dominant tradition inside evaluation often delivered evaluations based on qualitative ('soft') data which concentrated on educational processes rather than outputs. There was dissatisfaction too, with some of the major evaluation contractors who tended to deliver the same model to all their clients irrespective of their needs.

Despite these difficulties the concept of a *pilot* project, where ideas and strategies were being deliberately tried out was one that forced evaluation to the fore. This was aided by two other factors: first, the fact that TVEI encouraged teachers and lecturers to go and visit each others institutions to observe each others' practice; secondly, that with the extension of TVEI on the horizon teachers were increasingly asked about the results of the pilot project and what they believed they had learned. Project personnel, very often with the assistance of the evaluator, began to acquire the language and concepts of educational evaluation (and in many cases of education itself) which permitted them to have useful dialogues with each other. The model of 'teacher as evaluator' is particularly important and appropriate for the extension project where, because of the number of institutions involved, a self evaluation model is the only one possible. In my judgement one of the greatest successes of TVEI is the ways in which it has helped those teachers involved to become more self-reflective — for many it is the beginning of extended professionalism (Hoyle, 1969).

Conclusion

Managing change is one thing, institutionalising it so that it is part of education is another. The government is using the law to bring in the National Curriculum and it will be held there by the rule of law. The National Curriculum does not appear to be very 'TVEI friendly', with the exception of technology, but schools will have room to manoeuvre such that large elements of TVEI could be incorporated if they wished. Whether they will wish to do so once the supporting money has run out is a crucially important question. It will depend on whether there has been a genuine cultural change, a shift in values such that technical and vocational education is genuinely seen to be a full partner alongside academic education. Maybe the forces which will ultimately determine this lie in the parental market place.

If one looks inside the schools and colleges to see whether managerial structures are evolving which would support TVEI in the future one has to be disappointed. The National Curriculum must mean that much of TVEI will have to be delivered horizontally across the curriculum, e.g. profiling, economic and industrial awareness, information technology, work experience, enterprise. This will be difficult where the major organisational structures, the departments, are vertically organised. There are very few examples of schools developing and resourcing horizontal structures to support these developments, e.g. matrix organisations.

References

HARLAND, J. 1987, The TVEI experience: Issues of control, response and the professional role of the teacher. In D. GLEESON (ed.), *TVEI and Secondary Education: A Critical Appraisal*. Milton Keynes: Open University Press.

HELLER, J. 1980, *Good as Gold*. London: Corgi.

HOYLE, E. 1969, *The Role of the Teacher*. London: Routledge and Kegan Paul.

REVANS, R. 1981, *Action Learning*. London: Blond and Briggs.

RODWIN, V. G. 1984, *The Health Planning Predicament: France, Quebec, England and the USA*. Los Angeles: University of California Press.

MULTILINGUAL MATTERS LTD
Bank House, 8a Hill Road, Clevedon
Avon, England, BS21 7HH